JOY TO THE WORLD

Sara and John Lindsey Series in the Arts and Humanities

JOY TO THE WORLD

The Life and Paintings of Lu Ann Barrow

EDITED BY KATHLEEN DAVIS NIENDORFF

Texas A&M University Press
College Station

First edition

This paper meets the requirements of ANSI/NISO Z39.48-1992 (Permanence of Paper).
Binding materials have been chosen for durability.
Manufactured in China by Martin Book Management

Library of Congress Cataloging-in-Publication Data

Names: Niendorff, Kathleen Bailey Davis, editor. | Barrow, Lu Ann. Paintings. Selections.
Title: Joy to the world: the life and paintings of Lu Ann Barrow / edited by Kathleen Davis Niendorff.
Other titles: Sara and John Lindsey series in the arts and humanities.
Description: First edition. | College Station: Texas A&M University Press, [2026] | Series: Sara and John Lindsey series in the arts and humanities | Includes index.
Identifiers: LCCN 2025050324 (print) | LCCN 2025050325 (ebook) | ISBN 9781648433580 (cloth) | ISBN 9781648433597 (ebook)
Subjects: LCSH: Barrow, Lu Ann. | Women artists—Texas—Biography. | Artists—Texas—Biography. | Texas—Intellectual life—20th century. | BISAC: ART / Individual Artists / Artists' Books | ART / American / General | LCGFT: Biographies.
Classification: LCC ND237.B268 J69 2026 (print) | LCC ND237.B268 (ebook)
LC record available at https://lccn.loc.gov/2025050324
LC ebook record available at https://lccn.loc.gov/2025050325

Published by Texas A&M University Press
John H. Lindsey Building, Lewis Street
College Station, TX 77843
www.tamupress.com

This book complies with the EU General Product Safety Regulation (GPSR) (Regulation (EU) 2023/988). For regulatory inquiries and product safety matters within the EU, contact our authorized representative:
Mare Nostrum Group B.V.
Mauritskade 21D
1091 GC Amsterdam
The Netherlands
Email: gpsr@mare-nostrum.co.uk
Website: https://mngbookshop.co.uk/

This publication has undergone a risk assessment and meets applicable safety standards. Traceability identifiers: ISBN, batch number, and publisher contact details are provided for compliance. No hazardous materials or components are included in this product.

The chapter entitled "Lu Ann Barrow's Paintings of Imagination and Experience," by James Housefield, was previously published in the 2006 exhibition catalog by Valley House Gallery, The Paintings of Lu Ann Barrow. *It is used here by permission of James Housefield and Valley House Gallery.*

For Lu Ann and those who loved her

JOY TO THE WORLD

Jane Michael

I wanna' dance down the aisle in
    a big red hat.
Jump with joy.
Clap your hands.
Clang those bells.
Crash the cymbals,
Celebrate!
    Celebrate like King David himself were here.
Blow the trumpet.
Everyone, sway with the choir,
Someone twirl that red banner
Rejoice!
Rejoice as if the new baby,
    The prodigal son
        The soldier
            has come home.
We are glitter!
We are confetti!

Wait.

We are Episcopalians
We are stained glass.
We are prayer books.
We are like my East Texas aunt, who, hearing Mariachis,
    said it was all she could do to keep from tapping her toes.

Our joy is not for a special day; it is every day.
A gentle joy that comes with the morning,
Flows through our lives,
Bringing grace and gratitude,
Persists through all trials.
It is the fruit of the Spirit that makes us
    view the world with wonder,
        rejoice when babies are baptized,
            delight in the laughter of a Nobel laureate

We are salt.
We are light.

Still,

What if just once, the word went out,
Come to church Sunday.
Wear red.
Don't forget your dancin' shoes.

CONTENTS

YES, JOY

An Introduction

On September 24, 2022, St. Matthew's Episcopal Church in Austin was the site of an art festival with an exhibit and evening performance celebrating the life and work of longtime parishioner and well-known artist Lu Ann Barrow. Lu Ann was born July 19, 1934, grew up in Rosenberg, Texas, came to Austin to go to college, and settled here with husband David after his military duty. She died in Austin on July 25, 2020, after a brief illness (the pandemic prevented holding an event until 2022). Widely respected and collected, Lu Ann's work was exhibited regularly at the iconic Fiesta at Laguna Gloria Art Museum in Austin as well as in shows around the state. Her credits include designing a poster for the Texas Book Festival and serving as the featured artist at the first National Book Festival in Washington, DC, in 2001.

Always an independent type, Lu Ann found her own way from the Methodist church of her childhood to the Episcopal church, joining a small congregation in nearby Richmond, Texas. After high school, she came to Austin to study art at the University of Texas, where her teachers included influential Texas masters like William Lester (1910–1991), and where the prevailing mode of the day was Abstract Expressionism. But, as art historian Karen Pope explains in her essay "Reflections," Barrow was determined to follow her own muse, and her artistic vision ran in a much more representational, even "vernacular" vein. After graduating with a degree in fine art and a minor in anthropology, in 1956 Lu Ann met and married a US Air Force officer named David Barrow, who had grown up a Baptist and whose degrees from the University of Texas were in architecture and business. As David recalls it, she simply announced they would be Episcopalians. After he finished his tour of duty, they finally got to go on a honeymoon, a gift of David's father, to western Europe and Turkey. It was but the first of many, many trips abroad.

In fact, the impact of her travel on Lu Ann's work is very apparent. She loved the Middle East: shop scenes from Istanbul, the outdoor markets in Israel, the elegance of certain Egyptian women—all were fodder for her imagination. Likewise, she

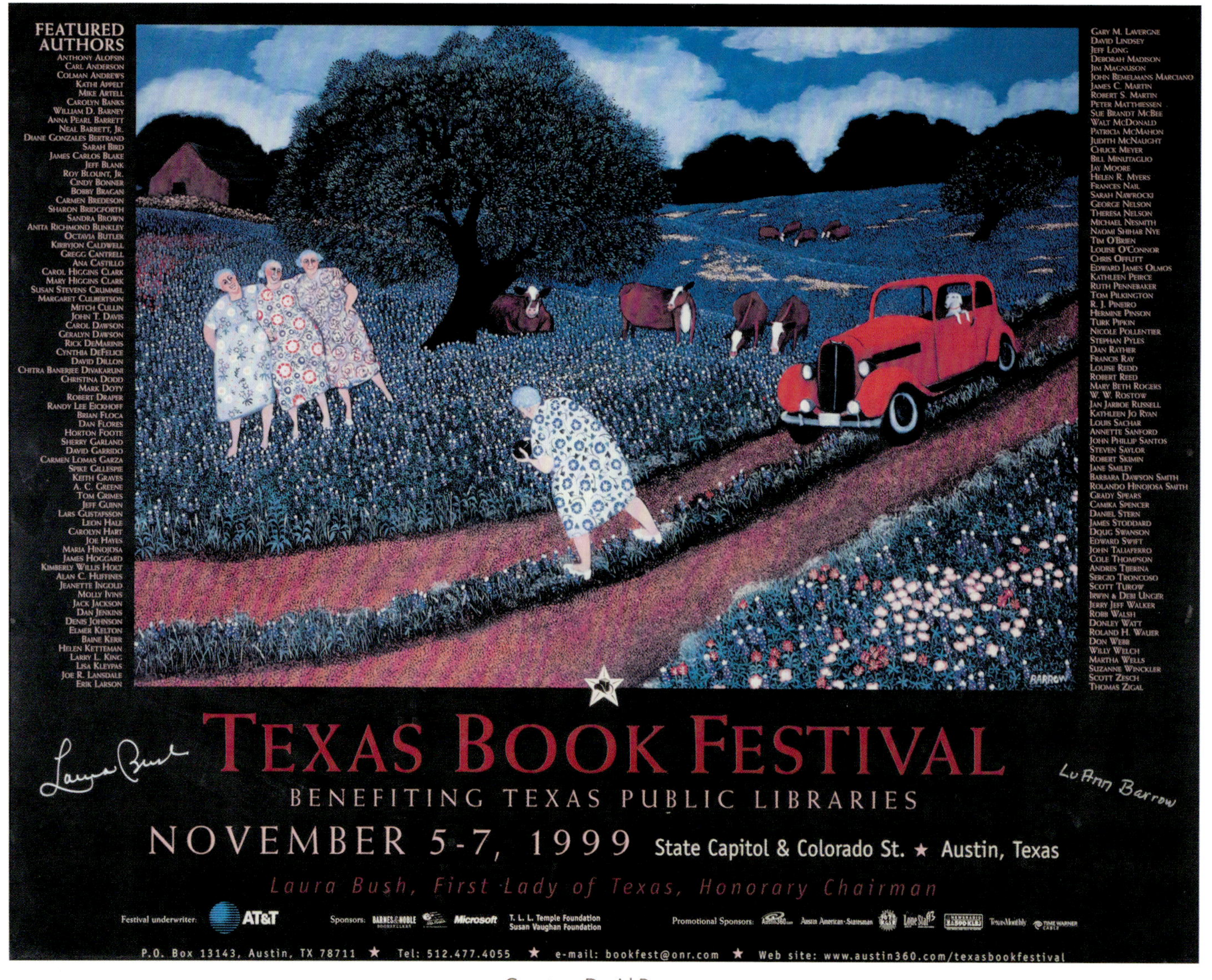

Courtesy David Barrow.

adored the folk art of Mexico. Indeed, although there is an occasional nod to elegance—such as an image of ladies at tea or the interior of a shop with a thousand neckties—most of her work depicts ordinary folk doing mostly ordinary things of daily life. As a kind of visual cultural anthropologist, Lu Ann abundantly displays in her work her interests, observations, and delight in her subjects.

Lu Ann also took great joy in depicting the life and passions of Black people, and she especially loved Black gospel music. Not surprisingly, the theme of the festival and celebration of her life at St. Matthew's Episcopal Church was "Oh Happy Day," a song that became popular in its 1969 adaptation by the Edwin Hawkins Singers. Lu Ann's painting by the same title depicts a line of Black worshippers, singing as they march along a trail through a forest of pine trees, a small white church in the background. Indeed, a number of Lu Ann's most popular works draw their subjects from African American culture and society, many of them underlining themes of home, family, and faith.

Faith plays an outsize role in the work of Lu Ann Barrow. As Pope's essay makes clear, Lu Ann's depictions of familiar biblical themes and stories "in the present tense" have drawn more admirers to her art than perhaps any other single aspect of her painting. One sees the Good Samaritan dressed in the coveralls of an auto mechanic, rushing to help a roadside victim, while in the background a parson rides stiffly on, ignoring the plight of the one who needed help. Jesus, wearing a straw hat and bib overalls, sits on a wooden crate beneath a tree and teaches his twelve disciples, while Mary, in a blue pinafore and white apron, listens in. Her sister Martha stands disapproving by the front porch of the farmhouse. As Pope's essay states, "The presentation of biblical subjects as current-day genre pictures recalls the tactic of those Old Masters" that connects Barrow's painting "to great art of the past." It also powerfully connects her work to her modern viewers.

The festival at St. Matthew's included some forty-one original works by Lu Ann Barrow, exhibited in the undercroft of the sanctuary, an afternoon reception and browsing, and an evening performance that featured instrumental and vocal solos, original poems, and the church's rector emeritus, Chuck Huffman, and his daughters singing from the album *Love Letter to St. Matthew's.* The event culminated with a performance by the St. James Missionary Baptist Church choir. For their final song, "Oh Happy Day," the choir invited a sanctuary full of Episcopalians and visitors to get out of their seats and march around the sanctuary, singing and clapping with the choir. For all those who witnessed it, this was indeed a happy day, and those who knew Lu Ann knew she would have loved it. Meanwhile, the relatively new rector of the church stood at the back, watching in near awe.

Presented in this book are pictures of most of the paintings from the festival, along with a number of others sold over the years by Valley House Gallery in Dallas, where Lu Ann's work was represented for more than three decades. Included also are a few owned by dedicated fans of her work who learned of this book and asked for inclusion of the pieces they own.

The first tribute encountered in the book, "Joy to the World," by poet Jane Michael, offers a joyful assessment, in verse, of Lu Ann's work and its central message to those of us who knew and loved her and also to those who will know her only through the art she left us. After this introduction, readers will find a personal statement written by Lu Ann in 2003, reflecting on her art, her experiences, and her "storytelling" approach.

Four essays are also included to further our understanding of this person and her life and work. The first, mentioned above, is "Reflections," by Karen Pope, retired faculty of the Allbritton Art Institute at Baylor University. Karen's essay illuminates Lu Ann's artistic expression in terms of the history of artistic expression, especially that of the twentieth century—that is, how she found her own idiom and boldly practiced it.

The second essay, "Artist to Artist: Questions I'd Like to Ask Lu Ann Barrow," was written by Ginger Henry Geyer, a practicing artist and occasional faculty member at the Seminary of the Southwest in Austin. Geyer has exhibited widely with her three-dimensional and, lately, two-dimensional works, which, like Lu Ann's, most often have a religious or spiritual underpinning. She also knowledgeably illuminates Lu Ann's method and technique. Lu Ann worked almost exclusively with oil on canvas, which she prepared—rather uniquely—with a black gesso background, in contrast to most painters, who begin with a white or neutral canvas. Geyer fittingly describes this practice of Lu Ann's as "bringing light out of darkness," a very apt metaphor for Lu Ann's approach to her work—and her life.

The third essay, "Blessings: Lu Ann's Vision of the Kingdom," is by the Reverend Susan Barnes, PhD, MDiv, a retired Episcopal priest and former museum director and art historian. And here we begin to realize Lu Ann's extraordinary ability to "translate" Bible stories into contemporary settings. Growing up in Richmond, Texas, in the coastal plain, Lu Ann knew country living firsthand: she saw farmers, horses and mules, wagons, and haymaking and likely witnessed quilting parties, picnics, barn dances, and so forth. All of these events are captured in Lu Ann's idiom and given spiritual significance that belies their "naïve" appearance. Even people who have never read the Bible can learn stories and lessons from the paintings alone.

The fourth essay, "Soul-Journers," offered by Cheryl Vogel of Valley House Gallery & Sculpture Garden, is by the dealer who represented Lu Ann and her work for some thirty years. It is an essay about the artist and her life, but it also tells the

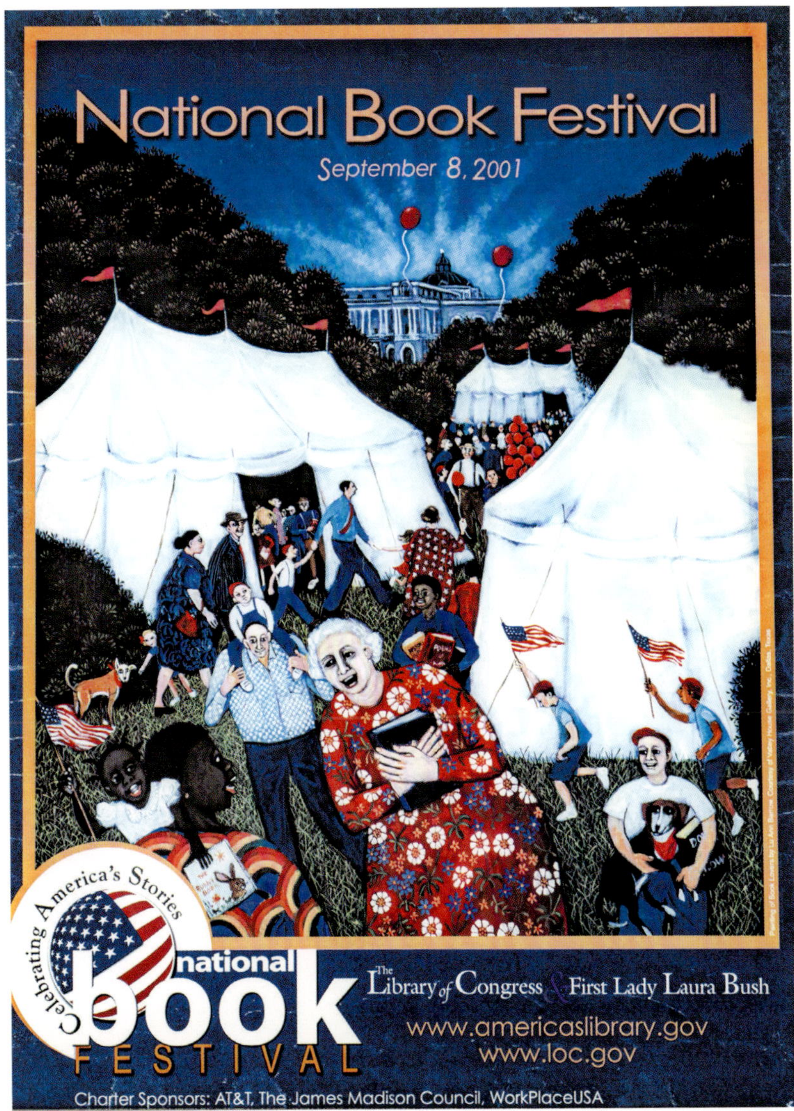

Courtesy David Barrow.

story of a friendship. As Vogel explains, when you show your soul in your art and discuss it with a person, that friendship becomes both profound and dear.

The essay by curator and art historian James Housefield, "Lu Ann Barrow's Paintings of Imagination and Experience," was prepared for a catalog, published by Valley House Gallery & Sculpture Garden to accompany the 2006 exhibition of Lu Ann's work, *The Paintings of Lu Ann Barrow*, which appeared at the Austin Museum of Art, the Longview Museum of Fine Arts, and Valley House. Housefield provides a thoughtful tour of the emotional, spiritual, and artistic landscape that surrounds Lu Ann's work.

A gallery of Lu Ann's paintings is followed by a very personal piece that provides the second "bookend" to this work. "Remembrance," written by Lu Ann's husband, David, offers his reflections on their life together and provides a valuable perspective on Lu Ann's approach to her work. His affection for Lu Ann—and her affection for her art and the life she and David built together—are apparent.

Of course, what runs through virtually every single painting, whether it is the scenery, the color, the people and animals, or even the facial expressions of the subjects, is the overweening notion of joy. As Housefield notes in his essay,

> Barrow's painted world embodies joy. Filled with laughter and friendship, it is a world in which the patterns of everyday life are cause enough for celebration. "I can't do a painting that's not celebratory," Barrow says with a smile . . . the sense of joy expands as it becomes increasingly social. A love of . . . work and the relationships with people and animals . . . give [Barrow's figures] cause for celebration. Everyday activities like sewing, shopping, talking, and gardening contain their own purpose, satisfaction, and joy in Barrow's world.

There's joy in meeting up with African Christians at the church in Cana; there's joy in watching a little dog dance; there's joy in the Good Samaritan running to rescue the fellow in the ditch. There's joy.

Hence the title of this book, which is also the title of one of her works, is *Joy to the World.* And, as her friend, I can testify that Lu Ann Barrow was exactly that.

JOY TO THE WORLD

ARTIST'S STATEMENT

Lu Ann Barrow (1934–2020)

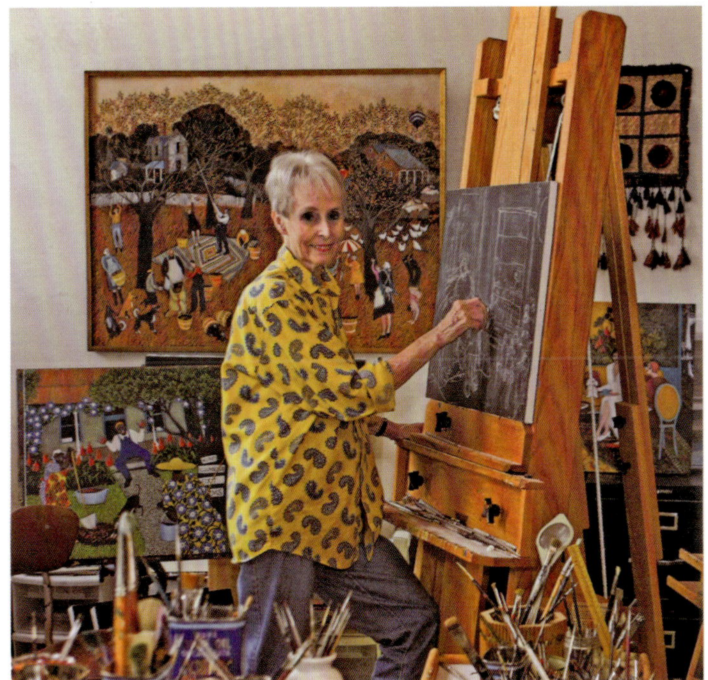

Lu Ann Barrow at work in her studio, 2006. Courtesy Valley House Gallery & Sculpture Garden.

Since graduating from the University of Texas with a degree in applied art, where I was fortunate to study under William Lester and Dan Wingren, I have exhibited in shows in Texas, Oklahoma, and New Mexico as well as numerous group and solo shows. My paintings have been used to illustrate two books, four book covers, and as posters for the Texas Book Festival in 1999 and the first National Book Festival in Washington, DC, in 2001. For the last ten years I have been represented by the Valley House Gallery in Dallas.

From my university days to the present, my paintings have been narrative in a folkloric style, using elements I've absorbed from childhood memories, from travels in Texas and the US, Europe, the Middle East, and Mexico, from observing people and listening to their stories, and from delighting in the presence of animals in our lives.

I usually begin a painting with a title, something I've read or heard that evoked an immediate image. For instance, hearing “too wet to plow,” I could visualize a farmer sitting on his tractor, playing a guitar while the rain comes down outside the barn door. Or “We had us a hallelujah time,” overheard in a checkout line as two ladies talked about an event at their church: I could immediately see the church, the surrounding grounds, the trees beyond, and the people celebrating as they boogied out of the church.

The tenor of my paintings is usually joyful and celebratory, with rare expressions of sorrow or even shadows.

I’ve tried using a subtle palette, but with the exception of some Middle Eastern desert scenes, my paintings are colorful, with a great deal of pattern and texture that people can identify with and that draw them into the painting and connect them to the story.

In the 1970s I took an intensive two-year course of Bible study that opened an inexhaustible source of ideas and images in my mind. The paintings I’ve done from scripture do not look “biblical” or different from my secular subjects, because I dress the subjects in clothes that are closer to our time in settings that are familiar to the viewer today. I think that secular and sacred are often seamless and that my biblical paintings are visual parables that must still work in regard to color and composition.

My Texas people are usually dressed in work clothes, are ordinary folks doing ordinary things, in a time frame somewhat earlier than today. The women would be in housedresses and aprons, the men in coveralls or work clothes. The figures seem to have small heads and elongated bodies, but this doesn’t become apparent to me until I’ve finished the painting.

I use animals, especially dogs, in most of my paintings because they seem to turn up in most of the stories I’m painting and because they speak to me. Even at the pyramids outside Cairo there were numerous curly-tailed mongrel dogs all over the surrounding grounds.

For me, painting is a language I’ve been blessed with and can use to gather what I’ve seen, read, heard, or experienced and share it with the viewer, a way to say visually, “Let me tell you . . .”

REFLECTIONS

Karen Pope

In the world of art history, it's fashionable these days to disparage "the canon" that has formed the basis for introductory courses and, for legions of students, a foundation framework for further investigation. By definition, a survey is selective and can't include everything, but every exploration must begin somewhere. Characterizing hunks of time and culture across the march of history, "key monuments" of the canon function as representatives of large bodies of work and act as examples of period styles, themes, and new directions.

When Lu Ann Barrow chose to pursue painting at the University of Texas in the early 1950s, the latest installment of the canon was Abstract Expressionism. This diverse, radical art, born in New York City, eschewed representation of the real world for autographic, gestural, large-scale works that sought profound content in response to the traumas of World War II and the emerging mantra of radical, existential self-expression. From the vantage point of the canon, Abstract Expressionism was the important art being produced in that decade. The University of Texas Art Department put away the classical casts that had facilitated the tradition of idealized figure drawing and embarked on what's now called "mark-making." In this context, Lu Ann Barrow may have been stubbornly devoted to representation or adventurously independent of the abstraction that must have been percolating in the studios. She certainly did not fall in line with this dominant trend or its successor, Pop Art. Represented by Pollock and Rothko in the 1950s and Rauschenberg and Warhol in the 1960s, these movements did not conquer Lu Ann's "different drummer," and we are all the richer for that difference.

A lifetime's devotion to witty and joyful depictions of lives in observed and remembered places now communicates a wonderful sense of confidence and self-directed devotion to an artistic voice that was distinctly unlike the prevailing dynamics in her university experience. Her chosen direction may have benefited from the tutelage of UT art professor William Lester (1910–1991), a Texas Regionalist painter committed to representation in the spirit of American Scene painting. Lu Ann, widely traveled and with Bible study a life practice, crafted a uniquely engaging and direct style. The easy legibility of her images is complemented by her technique: clear drawing, a bright palette, and brushwork that celebrates crisp detail. The strength conveyed by the directness of her style resembles the directness of the folk art collections displayed in her home.

My acquaintance with her work started with a display of paintings in a country club dining room. Because the show began around Valentine's Day, Lu Ann painted a large new work that she called *Love in Bloom*. In this painting, a couple enjoy a picnic on a blanket in a field of bluebonnets. A proffered apple invites the viewer to see the simple event as a contemporary temptation in a modern-day Eden.

Ultimately, what charms the viewer and has attracted many admirers is her ability to see and depict biblical stories in the present tense. As she has said, "Scripture is often more immediate than the literal time frame of the biblical times." Indeed, her paintings visualize biblical stories in a vernacular so loving and witty that recognition of the picture's subject may dawn on the viewer only gradually. Old Masters depicted the event of *Mary and Martha* and their contrasting responses to Christ's presence in their home by visualizing Martha, busy at work in a cluttered kitchen, while Mary sits at the feet of Jesus, all figures clothed in the costumes of the artists' times. Mary seems to leave all the important hospitality of the occasion to her sister while she listens to the visitor. The reader of the story learns which of the two reactions to Jesus's visit is the more important. In Lu Ann's lifelong attention to the Bible's stories, her imagination visualized the event in her own times, too; often the setting is the Texas countryside, where farm families in overalls have relaxed from their labors. In Barrow's *Mary and Martha,* a fellow is perched on a stump beneath an immense golden tree. He is clothed in the same white shirt and dark overalls as are worn by the twelve men lounging on the fall grass around him. Two dogs are sprawled among the men, whose hats have been set aside as they listen. Off in the right distance are fresh corn shocks that suggest the men under the tree are resting from the labor of the harvest. Among them, a female figure sits in a pose of rapt attention, her hands in her lap on her clean apron. The assembly sprawls across the front half of the picture space. In the background (scale not terribly important) stands the other female figure, wiping her hands on her apron as she stands remote from the group near her Texas porch and rockers; she obviously has been working in the house. The immense shrubbery near her supports what looks like a large lacy tablecloth, an attribute signifying her excellent hospitality skills. The details divert and delight—there is so much detail, the patterns conjure the artist's meticulous technique, the colors are vibrant, and the figures appear so realistically focused on the event at hand. Viewers imagine themselves as observers in this country setting and experience the delight in recognizing that the painting's title refers to *the* Mary and Martha, the sisters of the Bible story. Here, Jesus is one of the harvesters and the sisters wear country dresses and full aprons. The artist has recast an ancient story into a vivid tableau in relatable terms, a picture that is delightful as a purely secular image but is endearing and memorable as a "modern" interpretation of an old story.

The presentation of biblical subjects as current-day genre pictures in fact recalls the art historical period we call Baroque, when painters helped viewers involve themselves in biblical subjects by presenting them as events in contemporary settings and costumes. That perception gives me tremendous satisfaction as an art historian, because in this view, Lu Ann Barrow is an artist who found a new, personal idiom, which, in its innovation, connected her painting to great art of the past.

ARTIST TO ARTIST

Questions I'd Like to Ask Lu Ann Barrow

Ginger Henry Geyer

As an Austin artist one generation behind Lu Ann Barrow, I've always looked up to her. We shared the same gallery, Valley House, in Dallas. We both worked in highly detailed styles that directly engaged biblical stories and other narratives. She painted, I made painted sculpture, and on occasion we got to talk shop, comparing notes about tiny paintbrushes. I regret that I never visited her home studio, as such spaces are fascinating incubators of the creative spirit. All the stuff hanging around for no good reason, the stops and starts of half-finished works, the wondrous smell of paint, the play of light, the contrast of folk art collectables jumbled into a minimalist space—all of it contributes to a special atmosphere that propels the artist forward.

Lu Ann's studio practice was playful, but you can bet that it was also disciplined. No artist produces such a prolific, uniform body of work without sticking with it over time. I wish I had quizzed her about her technique, as an artist's method of working is like a metaphor for their very being. From close looking at her paintings I observe that she perfected the traditional medium of oil on canvas in her own way. Her choice of medium is curious, though, as the way she painted is more suited to a hard panel surface than to a stretched canvas. With fabric there is a give and take, brushstrokes have a spring to them, and the painting process becomes something of a dance. For precise work, control is necessary; I just wonder whether Lu Ann danced around while she painted. She did not engage the spontaneity of wide brushwork or blending, which are features of greasy oil paint. Nor did she scumble over dry surfaces or paint with layers of glaze. Dramatic light and shadow—that is, chiaroscuro—was not part of her sensibility. Bright acrylics could do the job, but they render a surface rather plastic. She chose oils for a reason: they glow.

"Facture" is the term for how the surface of a painting looks and feels, both in its brushwork texture and in its sheen. Facture is what you cannot enjoy in a photograph of a painting—the mysterious depth of a dark space, the buildup of paint for a burst of light, the playful little twists that reveal the artist's hand. Especially in Lu Ann's work it is interesting to decipher where one color is layered over another or reveals the dark behind it. Seeing in person lets you enjoy where a swath of dots pulsates in a flattened plane, with delightful raised points—that is, impasto. Lu Ann had an arsenal of signature brushstrokes—e.g., her graceful foliage and swaths of dots. I imagine she was like a needlepointer happily lost in her repetitive work. Mark-making is a human response to being alive, and I wonder how she made the dots—with brushes or Q-tips, or sticks dipped in paint such as Aboriginal artists used? Something about her patterns harks back to such symbolic, "primitive" works even more than to the more genteel surfaces of the nineteenth-century French pointillists, where dots of color blend in the eye as you step away. Photographic pixels work the same way, but in grids. The big difference is that Lu Ann's facture is not mechanical. There are some tricky effect brushes that make several dots at a time, but there is no evidence of this, nor is it likely she dabbed on domes of paint from a nozzle bottle—unlike acrylics, oil paint doesn't come in squirt bottles. She probably wore out detail brushes in the same way the Twelve Dancing Princesses wore out their dancing slippers. And when the graceful points were worn down just so, these stubby brushes would be perfect for dotting. Why does this matter? Because visual arts are embodied in matter . . . the stuff of life that is blessed by creation and furthermore by the incarnation. Love itself is what caused the incarnation, that incredible notion that the spirit of God descends into the material world outfitted in flesh and blood in a particular time and place. Incarnation is at once pragmatic and mysterious. It relies on physicality, and the artist's choice of technique is intrinsic to the work.

Lu Ann boldly re-created this paradox of incarnation in the very way she began a painting: note the photo of her at the easel. She is freely sketching on a canvas, not meticulously detailing a settled composition. Key elements inspired by a title start it off, but during the course of painting, things evolve. This is one of the attributes that distinguishes art from craft—the artist does not necessarily know what the outcome will look like. There is no preconceived pattern to follow; the Spirit changes things. Notably, Lu Ann prepared her canvas with a black gesso ground—"ground" being the term for this initial layer from which all else will emerge. While this is not uncommon, most painters begin with a white or tinted midtone background. Lu Ann is literally bringing light out of darkness, as in the preamble to the Gospel of John. Colors set against black will pop. Shading is done by letting the black peep through rather than adding dark to light. The black is not obscured but is in service to the colors. This is most noticeable in facial features of her characters—they emerge rather than being imposed. They are "bodied forth," and this activates their humanity. Her figures sometimes feel formulaic, pinheads with elongated limbs, but they have an uncanny presence that prevents them from being mere illustrations. Presence evokes spiritual resonance; that is, it is at once in the present and memorable. The things we make can mediate God's presence to us.

A delightful technique Lu Ann used derives from as far back as sixth-century Byzantine art, where the patterned robes of the saints were rendered as flat cutouts, rather than naturally modulated to the body. Gustav Klimt also used this effect, and today we see it in figurative works of several contemporary Black artists. Patterns from African fabrics appear in Lu Ann's textiles, as well as handmade pioneer lace, braided rugs, and lush Turkish carpets. Patterns obviously necessitate repetition; as a devout Episcopalian, Lu Ann had repetitive ritual ingrained in her daily life. Those who know the mind-surpassing beauty of ritual can appreciate the influx of patterns that infuse each of Lu Ann's paintings. You can get lost in the details. For some it would be laborious to brush on detail after detail, but I'm betting that for Lu Ann it was meditative.

One thing just leads to another. One shape is distinguished from another, but look—she rarely used hard outlines. Permeable boundaries occur throughout, and she often maintained the size of an element rather than receding it into the background, as with traditional perspective tricks. For instance, see the lawn in *Noah's Ark* or the texture of snow in *Christmas in Front of the Church.*

As for subject matter, Lu Ann revels in telling an old story in a new way, something like the Jewish tradition of midrash. Biblical stories abound, but you'll notice she features the positive stories, none of the violence. In this jaded age of ours, joy is the hardest thing to depict in art. Joy must be grounded in authenticity before it can float off into bliss. Lu Ann excelled at that, probably because she was not sentimental about nostalgia. She simply enjoyed it. The charming naïveté of her paintings sometimes leads people to assume that she was an outsider artist, one who was untrained, a bit daft or reclusive, living on the margins and innocent of the pretensions of the art world. The difference is that her work is not raw, weirdly visionary, or roughly cobbled together. Lu Ann was sophisticated and not corny; she was formally trained, comfortable, and traveled a lot. She had more than her share of angst; perhaps that drew her to paint in such a cheerful, innocent style.

These days, we artists are subjected to the supersensitivity of cultural appropriation—that is, making artwork that mimics, exploits, and diminishes the significance of the expressions of a culture not our own. Cultural appropriation is a serious criticism of work made by privileged people who do not see the imbalance of power, especially when artwork reaches the

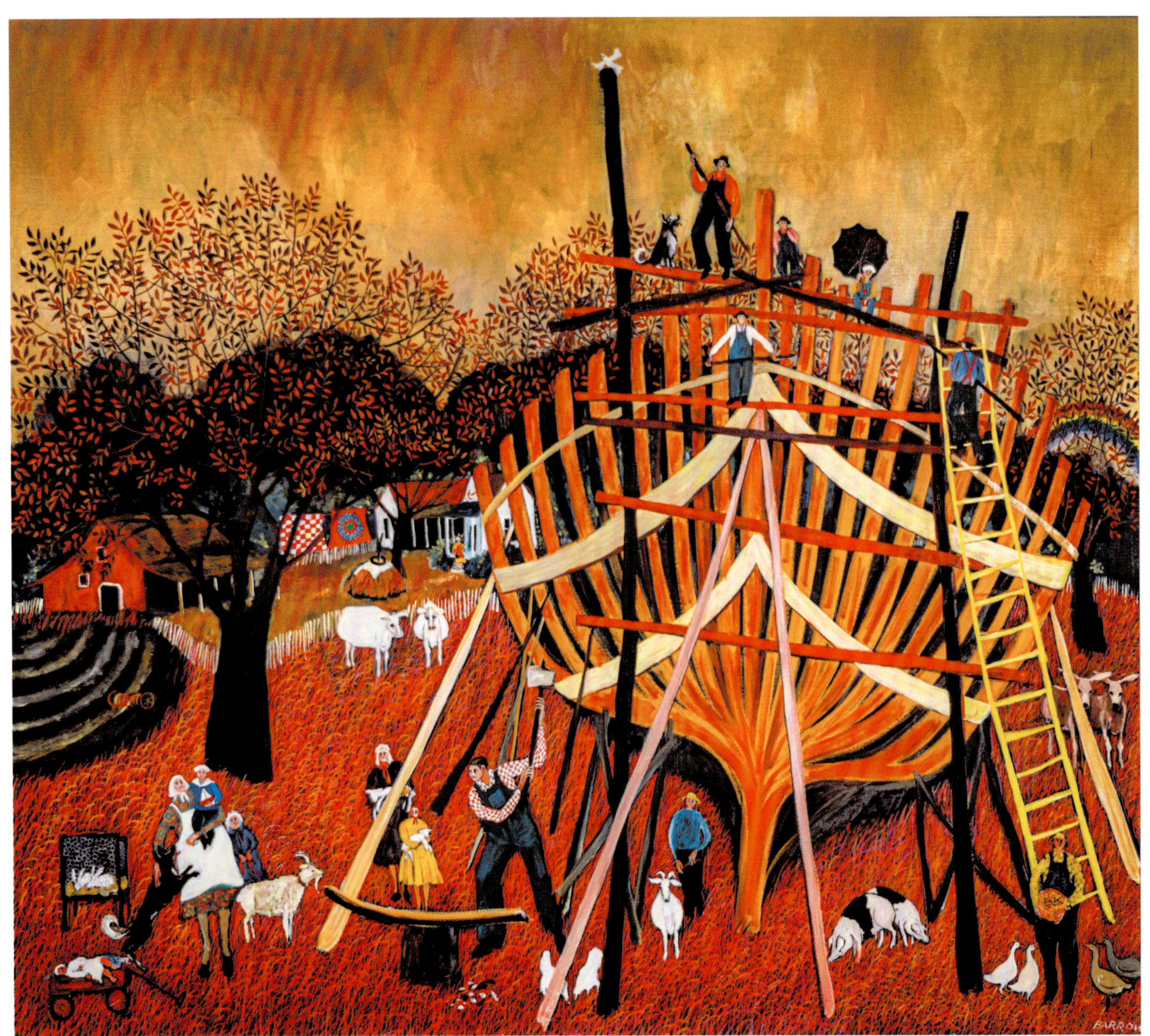

Noah's Ark, 1999, oil on canvas, 48 × 60 inches. Collection of David Barrow.

market. Lu Ann gleefully depicts her travels to underdeveloped countries a few decades ago. Today she might be challenged as benefiting from these foreign clichés. She notes that the body language of Black people projects more feeling, especially joy, than her own WASP restraint allows. When commissioned to create a poster for the 2001 National Book Festival, Lu Ann was cautioned to remove the "do-rag" bandanna from a Black figure. Many of us contend that there is a charm in such headwear, but others consider it derogatory. What appears to be celebratory to some may feel demeaning to others, and the artist will be called out. Surely over time such borrowings will lose their offensiveness, but we must also side with oppressed people of color who are flat-out weary of being stereotyped. Lu Ann does not cross this line, in my opinion. Her intentions were always good—she uplifts rather than denigrates; she celebrates other cultures as an appreciative outsider and invites us all to the party. She personally reveled in the hallelujahs, she revered the Day of the Dead, and she honored both rural foibles and citified teatime. The dark side of human emotion is unlikely to be suggested—no, she goes for the gold. Humor in her work is never mocking, and although humor is always culturally specific, she manages to let us laugh. What a relief. Just check out her 1989 *Big Snake*.

The last thing I'd like to ask Lu Ann is how she handled her latter years when she felt no longer able to paint. Artists don't retire in the traditional sense; the creative flow may be stunted, but it is an ever-present drive. How did she compensate? Her illness may have robbed her of her manual dexterity or vision, or perhaps energy level (again, physicality matters), but I wonder how she kept track of the barrage of fascinating images that would otherwise go into a painting. Knowing when to stop, to safeguard the quality of a body of work, is a huge achievement.

Lu Ann, like many artists, was hesitant to ascribe meaning to her work—what you see is what you get. There is no hidden symbolism, other than the occasional religious imagery such as the flabbergasting "Jesus face fabric," which she actually saw somewhere. Yet good artworks exist outside the artist's own intentions, and some interpretation can add to, rather than subtract from the viewer's experience. So, Lu Ann, forgive a fellow artist for imposing, both critically and admirably, upon your masterful body of work. However, when there is "much of a muchness," exuberance cannot be contained.

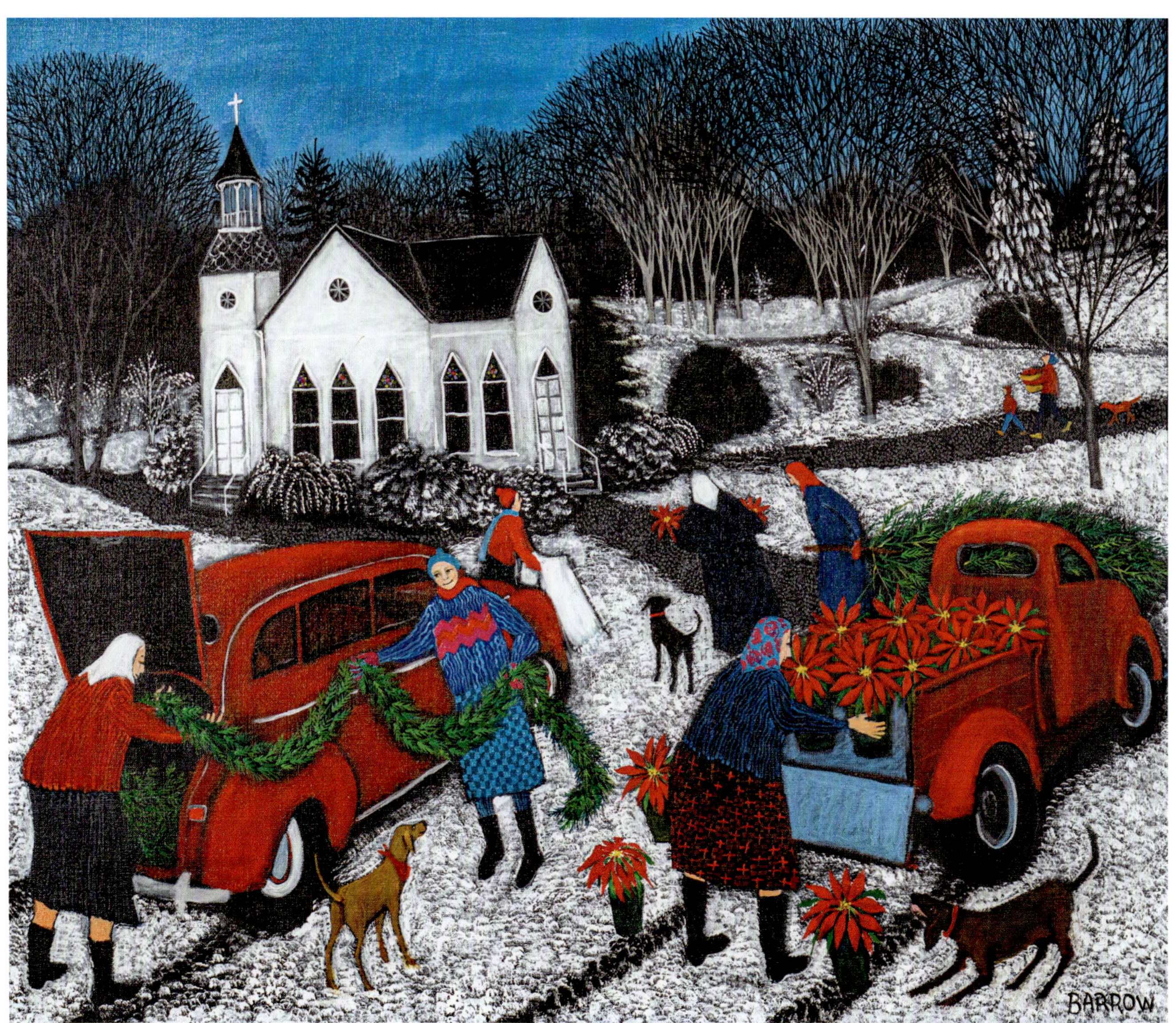

Christmas in Front of the Church, n.d., oil on canvas, 28 × 24 inches. Private collection.

BLESSINGS

Lu Ann's Vision of the Kingdom

Susan Barnes

One of the great blessings of my time as a priest at St. Matthew's was becoming friends with Lu Ann Barrow. Elegant, beautiful, and graceful, she embodied the Modernist esthetic of the handsome home that David had designed for them. She was also playful and had a sly wit. Her artistic taste was sophisticated, spirited, and wide ranging. She not only collected, she *embraced* folk art and Indigenous traditions: witness her installing her own magnificent, moving Day of the Dead altar at home, year after year.

It is rare for a painter to successfully translate biblical stories into their own day. Caravaggio did it well in Italy, around 1600. Lu Ann did, too, in her time. Her success is a testament to both the depth of her faith and the breadth of her artistic imagination. Using a humble, intentionally naïve style and setting her stories in the countryside or small towns with common folk as characters, she welcomed viewers of all kinds into the scenes.

Take the parable of the Good Samaritan (Luke 10:25–37). You recall that in the story a Jewish man has been robbed, wounded, and left to die alone on the side of a highway going up to Jerusalem. Two Hebrew holy men—a priest and a Levite—pass him by, fearful for themselves. But a Samaritan, whom Jews normally shun, stops to give first aid and then carries the man to an inn where he pays for the man's continued care. Rather than try to do a historical representation, which would be stilted and meaningless to all but a few, Lu Ann recast the story. Two expensive vehicles—one possibly driven by a parson—have passed the man by, but a simple auto mechanic stops to help. You don't have to know the gospel story to catch the fundamental point of Jesus's parable: love your neighbor and reach out to help the one in need.

Lu Ann translated the parable of the lost coin (Luke 15:8–10) directly to the present day in *Lost and Found*. Whether you know the story or not, you feel the celebration of the woman with her neighbors that she has recovered the coin she searched for so diligently.

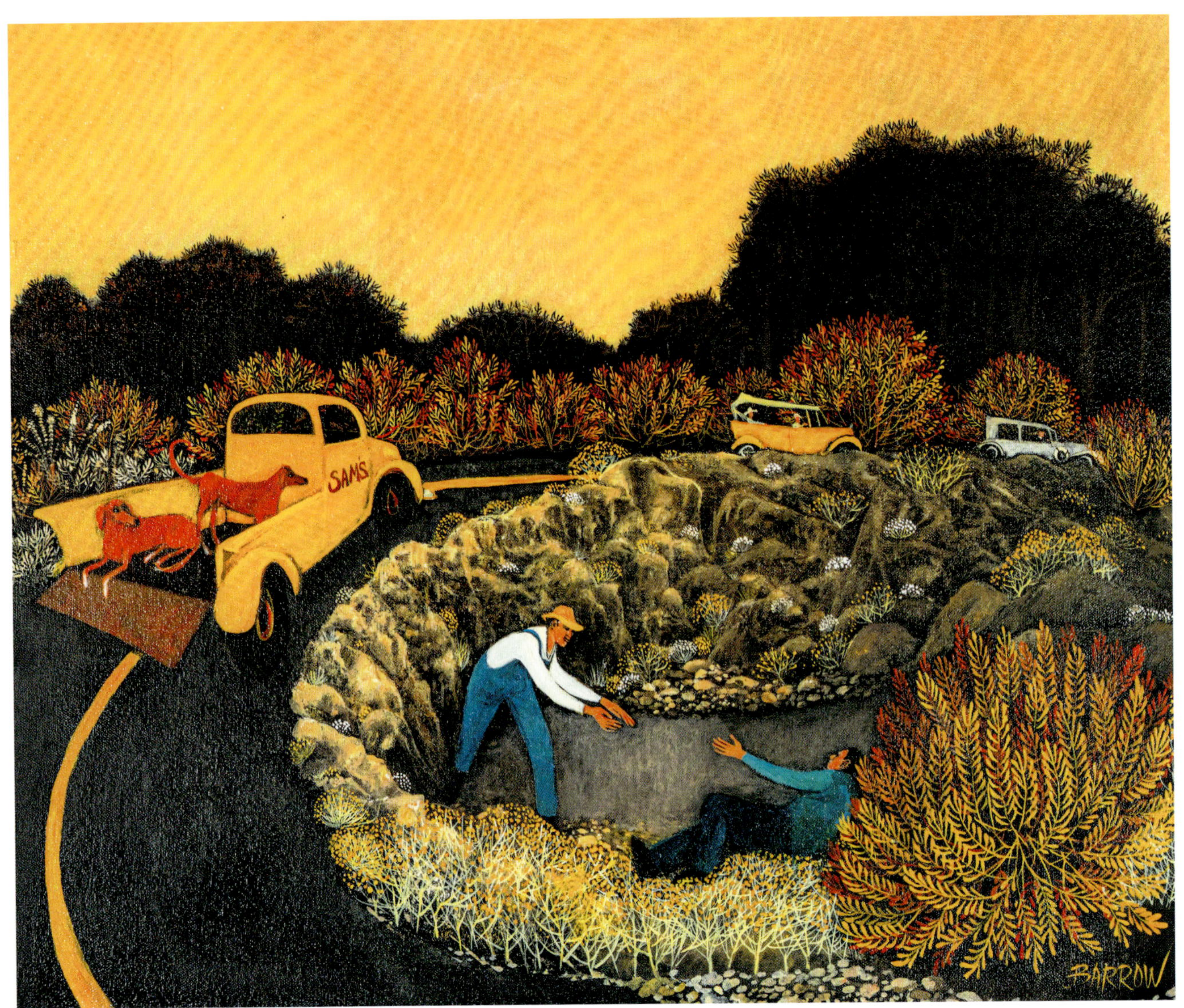

The Good Samaritan, n.d., oil on canvas, 20 × 24 inches. Private Collection.

In her biblical paintings Lu Ann did not shy away from God's punishment. *Sheep and Goats* is a gentle Last Judgment, but an explicit one: the farmer's gestures clearly mirror those of the risen Christ in countless Judgments down the centuries. In the main, however, Lu Ann shows Jesus as he embodies God's all-embracing mercy. *Even the Dogs* illustrates a remarkable moment in the gospels when Jesus changes his mind (Mark 7:24–30). Jesus had refused the plea of the Syrophoenician woman kneeling before him to heal her bedridden daughter. He had likened her to a dog, dismissing her as unworthy because she was a Gentile. Courageously the woman persisted, saying, "Sir, even the dogs under the table eat the children's crumbs." Lu Ann presents the moment when Jesus consents.

In her insightful essay, Ginger Geyer points out that by building up her paintings from a black primer ground, Lu Ann quite literally brought "light out of darkness." Indeed. Presenting gospel stories as she did, she brought to light their timelessness, and the truth that human beings have the same sins and virtues in all times and places.

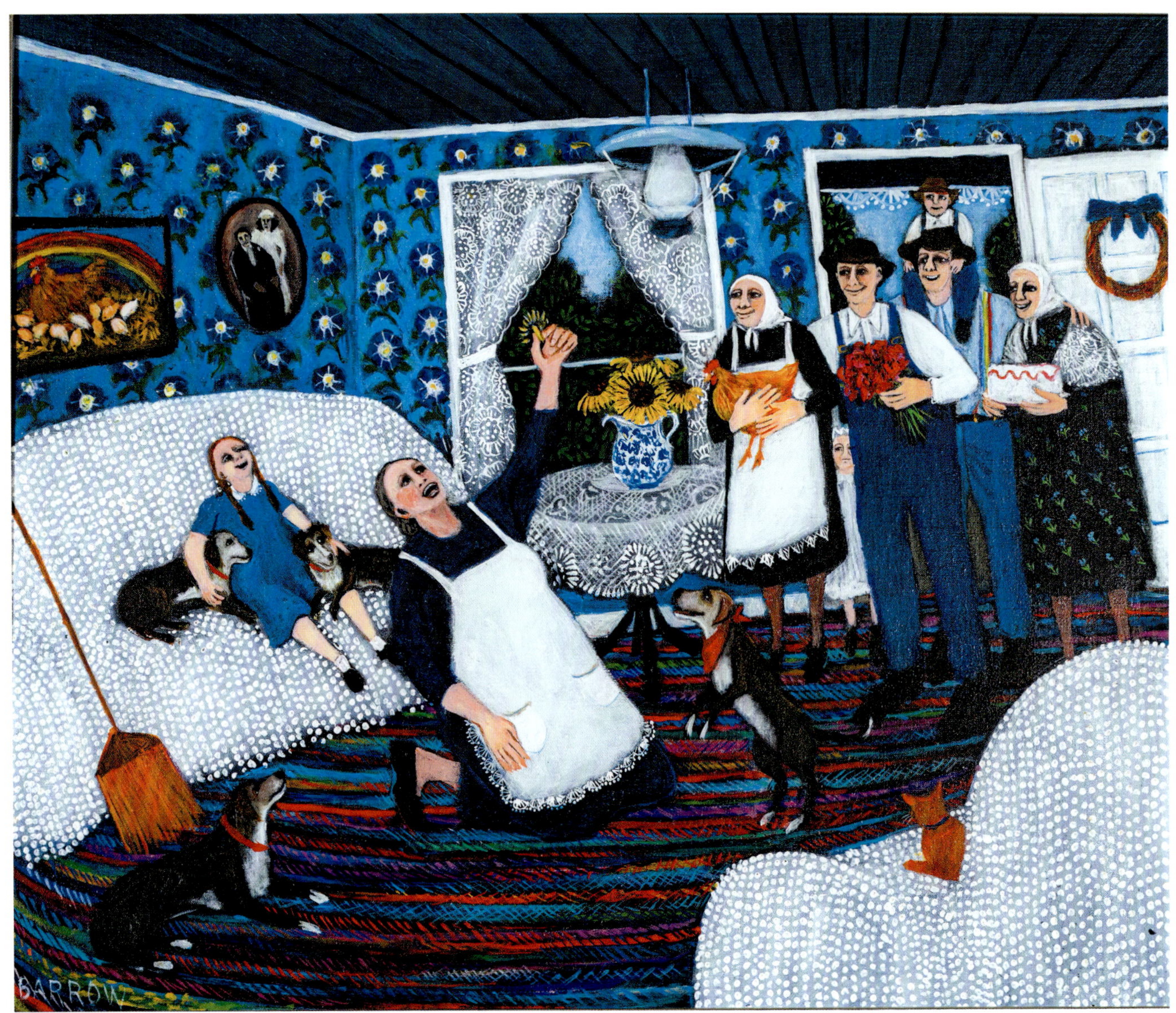

Lost and Found, n.d., oil on canvas, 21 × 25 inches. Private collection.

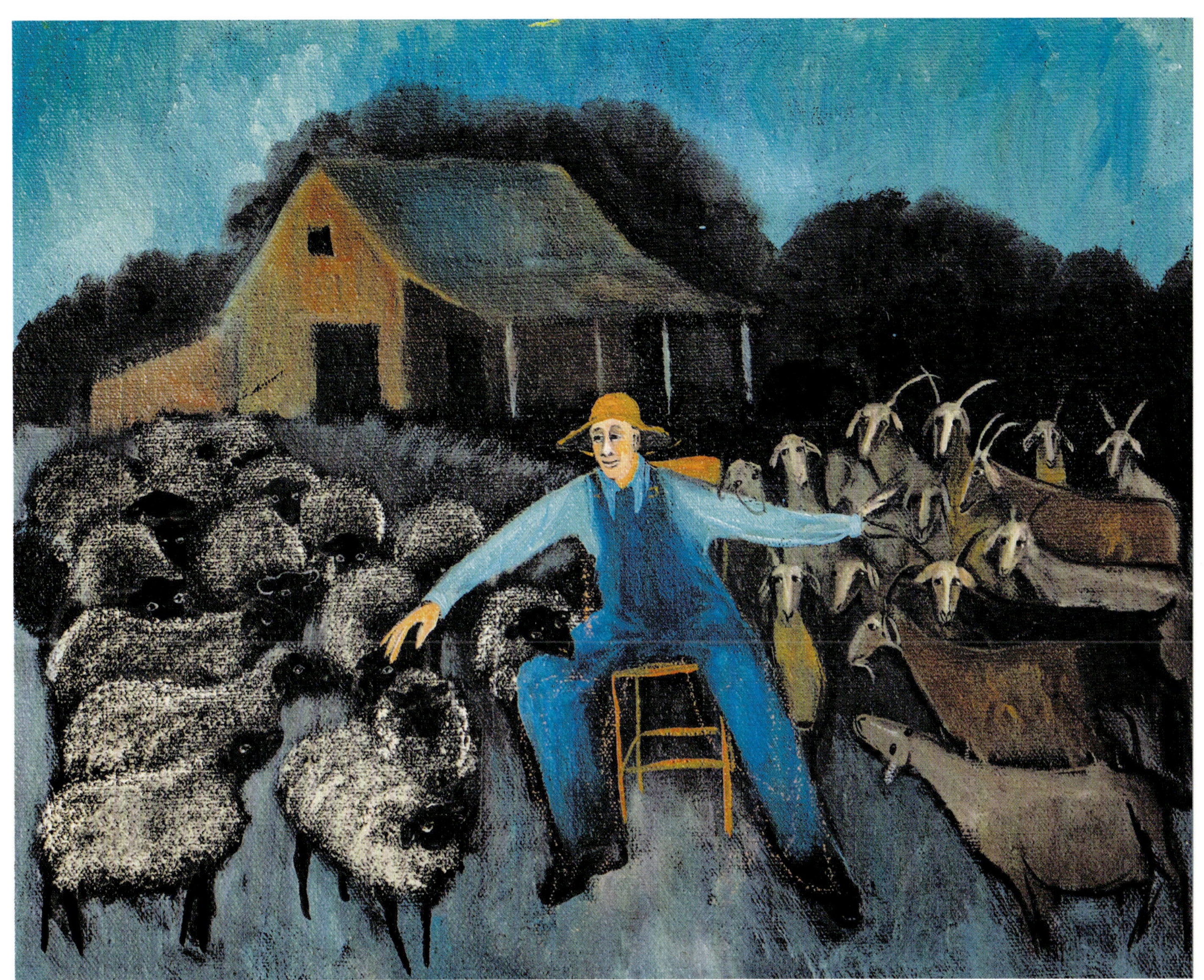

Sheep and Goats, n.d., oil on canvas, 11 × 14 inches. Private collection.

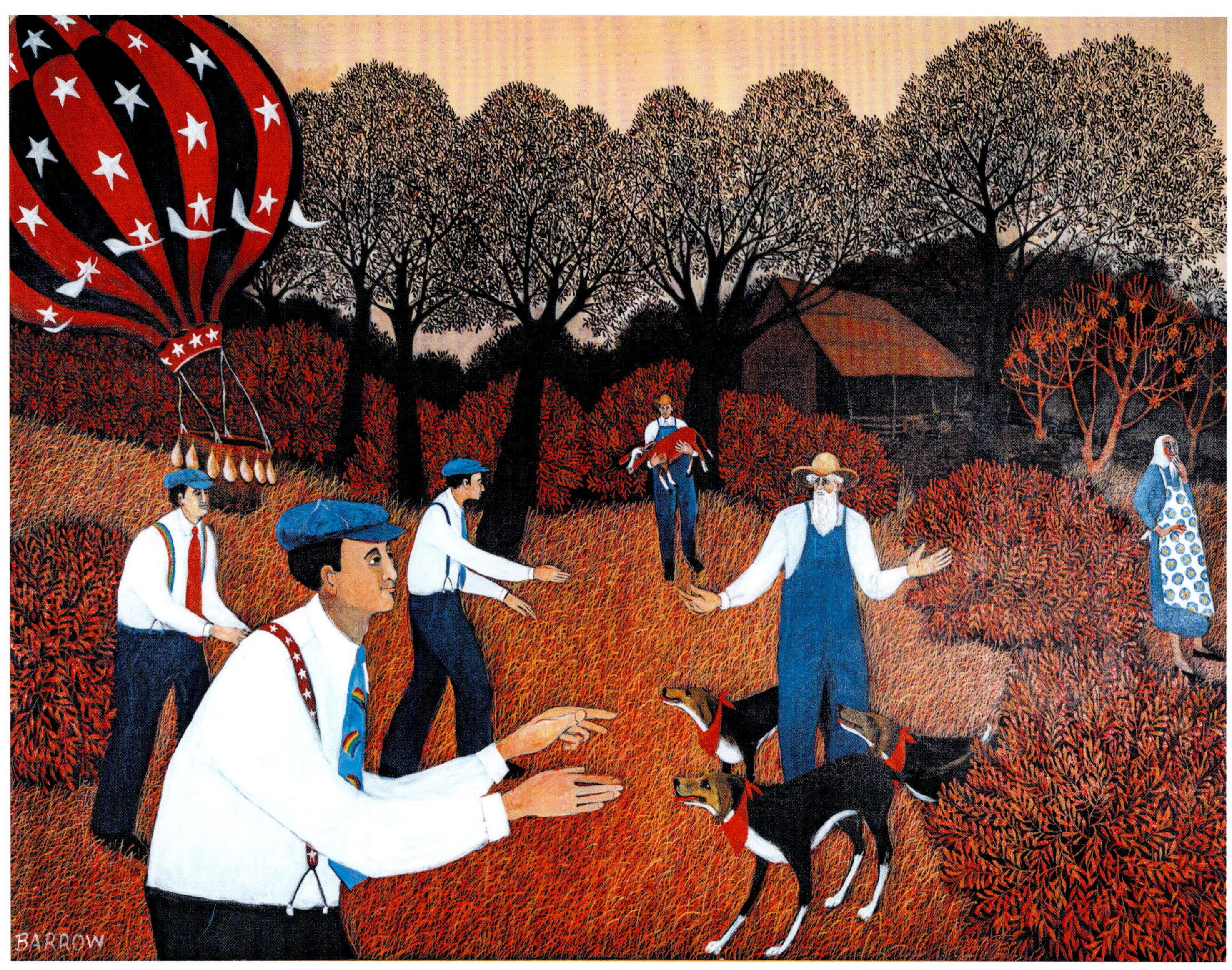

Even the Dogs, n.d., oil on canvas, 20 × 24 inches. Private Collection.

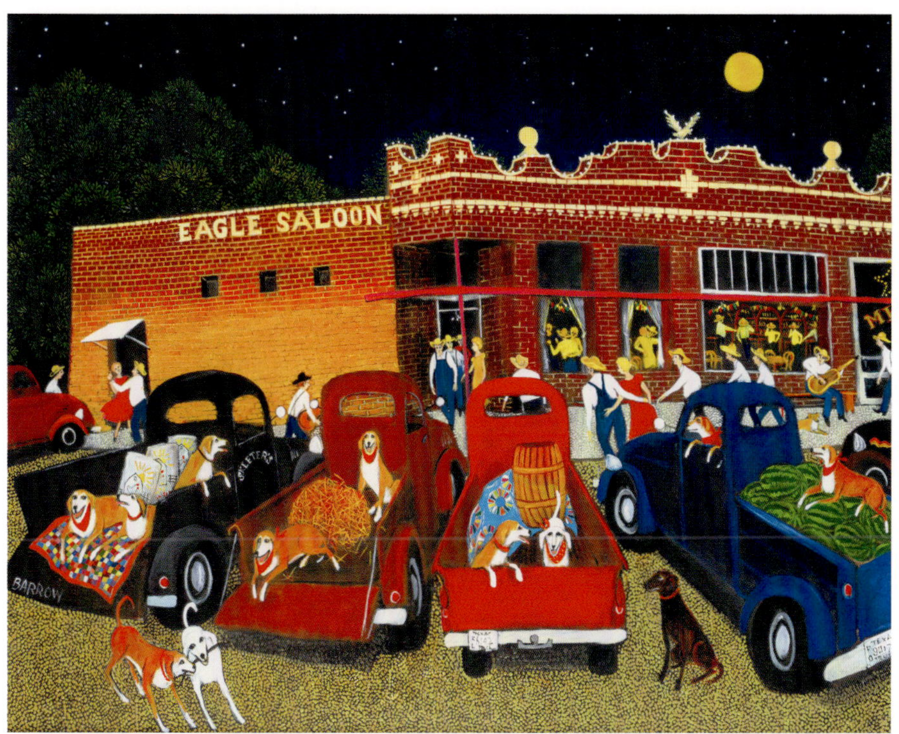

Honky Tonk Dogs in Front of the Eagle Saloon, 1999, oil on canvas, 24 × 30 inches. Private collection.

Lu Ann's paintings celebrate the light of life in community. It may be the joys of simple gatherings like those in *Honky Tonk Dogs in Front of the Eagle Saloon*. Or the strength of compassionate caring in *The Paralytic and His Friends*, where men have teamed up to carry an afflicted friend to the place where Jesus is healing all who come.

Morning Has Broken might first be taken as an everyday encounter. With a closer look we recognize it as a picture of the first Easter morning. The dove of the Holy Spirit soars over the three women who have come to the tomb to anoint Jesus's body. A halo of blue morning glories in bloom frames the darkness of the empty tomb. And two angels dressed in white and wearing rainbow suspenders greet them with the joyful news that He is Risen.

In this and in so many other paintings, Lu Ann shows us that God's Spirit is ever present, bringing joy, life, and blessing to us and to all of God's good creation.

The Kingdom of Heaven is here.

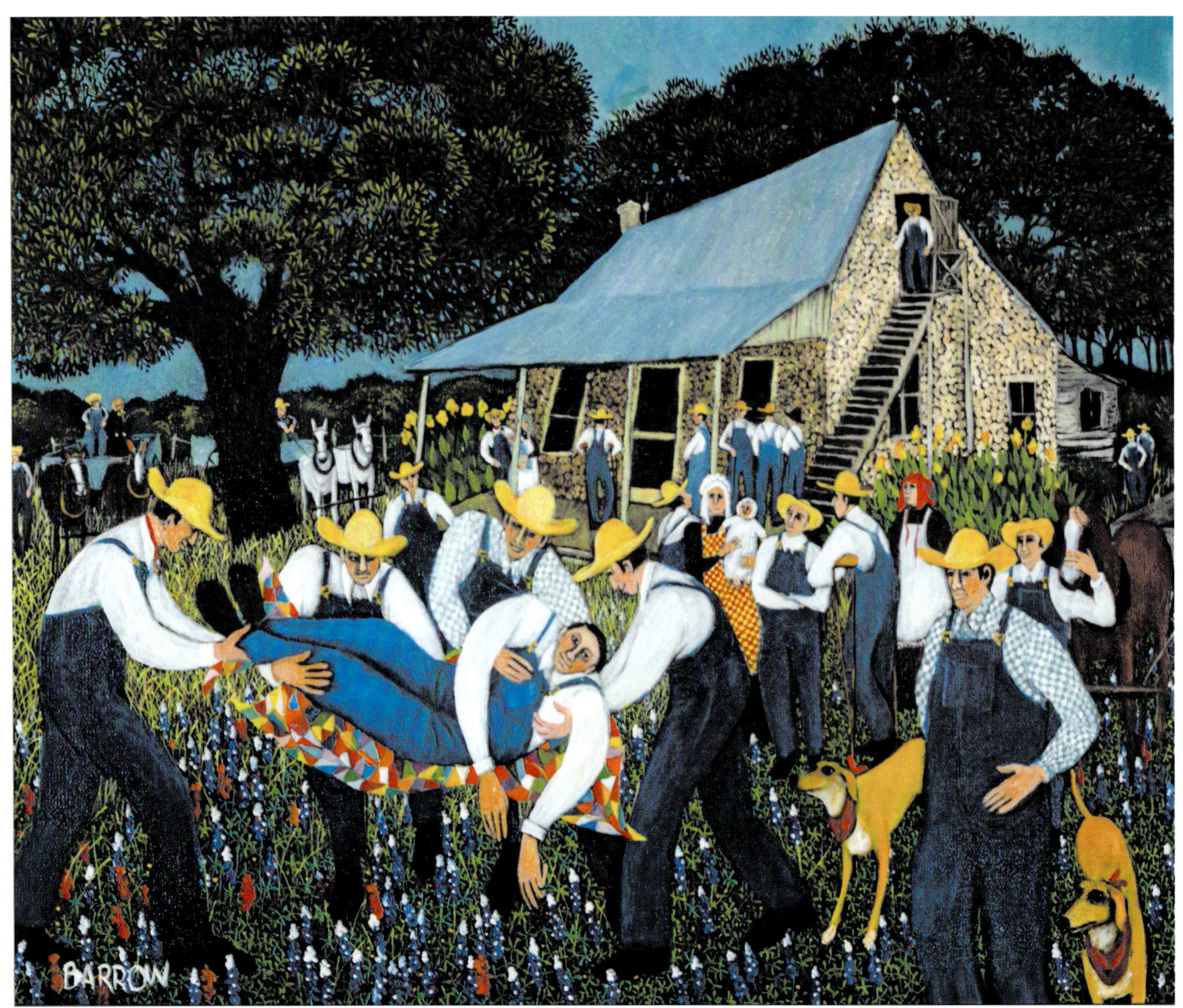

The Paralytic and His Friends, 1994, oil on canvas, 20 × 24 inches. Private collection.

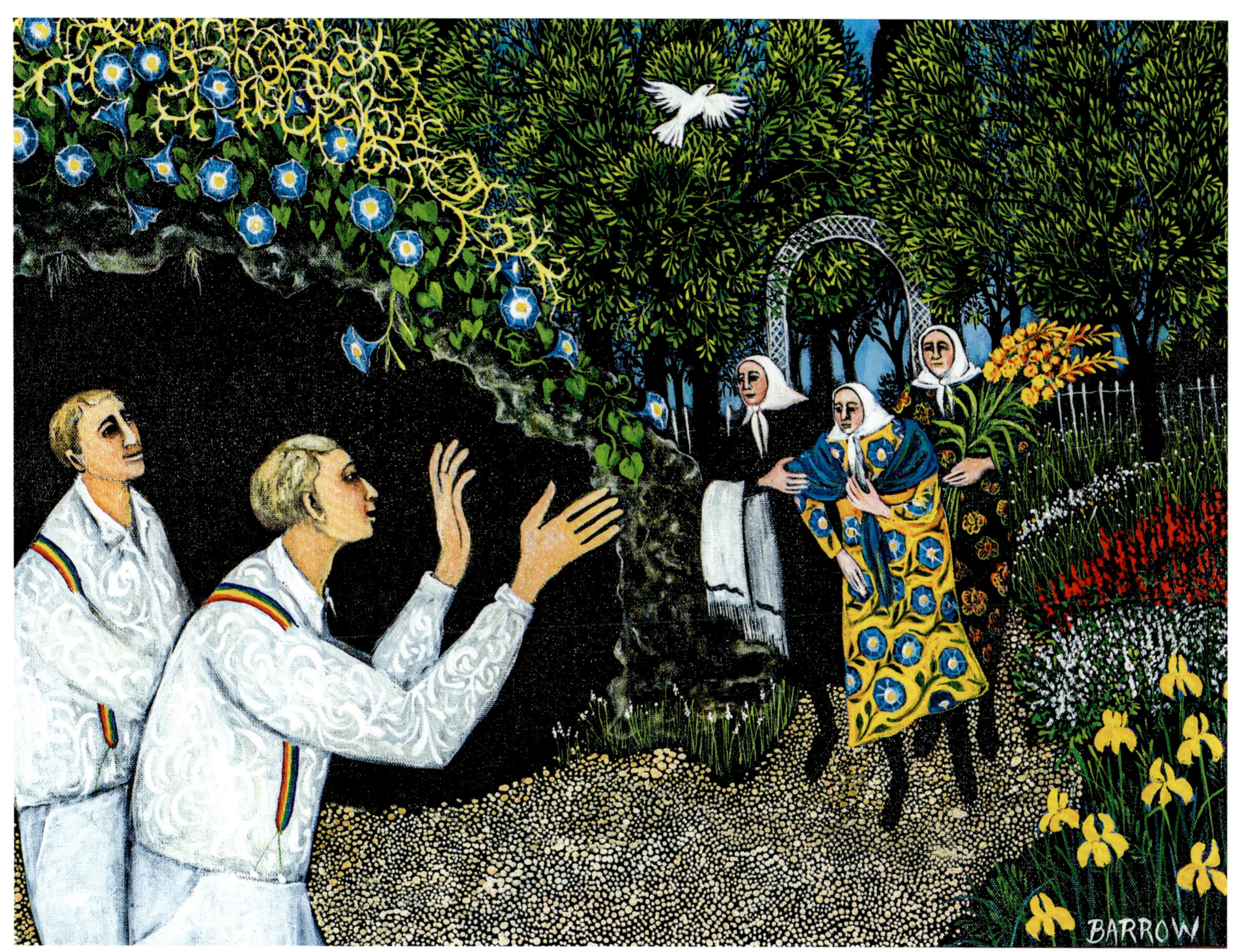

Morning Has Broken, n.d., oil on canvas, 29 × 35 inches. Private collection.

LU ANN BARROW

"Soul-Journers"

Cheryl Vogel

Lu Ann Barrow became part of our lives at Valley House Gallery in 1992 when she mailed us a black-and-white brochure from a twenty-five-year retrospective exhibition at Wunderlich Gallery in Austin. She sent it when she learned we were working with William Lester's estate. Lester was one of her favorite professors at the University of Texas at Austin, where she received a bachelor's degree in fine arts in 1956. Several other encounters with Lu Ann's paintings occurred, and I listened and contacted her. Our founder, the artist Donald Vogel, gave his enthusiastic blessing to my interest.

In an art world where so much art influences other artists, Lu Ann Barrow was an original. Her paintings came from observing the world around her, her love of people, and her faith. Her work was quite independent from the current directions in art and what she was taught at UT Austin. When I asked her about her college years, she told me a story that confirmed her confidence. After her professor Kelly Fearing told her that rose madder was not an appropriate pigment to use in art, she dressed up as a tube of it for a costume party that he also attended. She definitely had her own mind. She didn't hunger to go to museums. What she saw didn't sway her work, but a phrase overheard in a grocery store could immediately launch a visual image.

The focus of Barrow's subjects was threefold: biblical stories, rural Texas life, and her travels. The figures in her biblical paintings wore blue jeans and the dress of more recent times, giving the paintings contemporary relevance. Lu Ann recounted, "When I see an idea from scripture I seem to automatically 'see' the setting and figures in a different time frame, not necessarily today, but certainly in a more accessible time for the viewer. Therefore, the paintings do not 'look biblical.' I've always felt that the painting should stand on its own, whether the viewer recognizes the content and story or not." When Lu Ann taught a Bible study, she told me she would dress up like her subject. Jesus speaks to his disciples seated under a tree in *Mary and Martha*. The hero of *The Good Samaritan* is the driver of Sam's Pickup 24 Hour. Onlookers line the creek banks where Lydia is half submerged in *The Baptism of Lydia*. Adam and Eve appear in *Big Snake*, a roadside attraction. A young boy sitting on top of the bones of *Noah's Ark* is holding an umbrella.

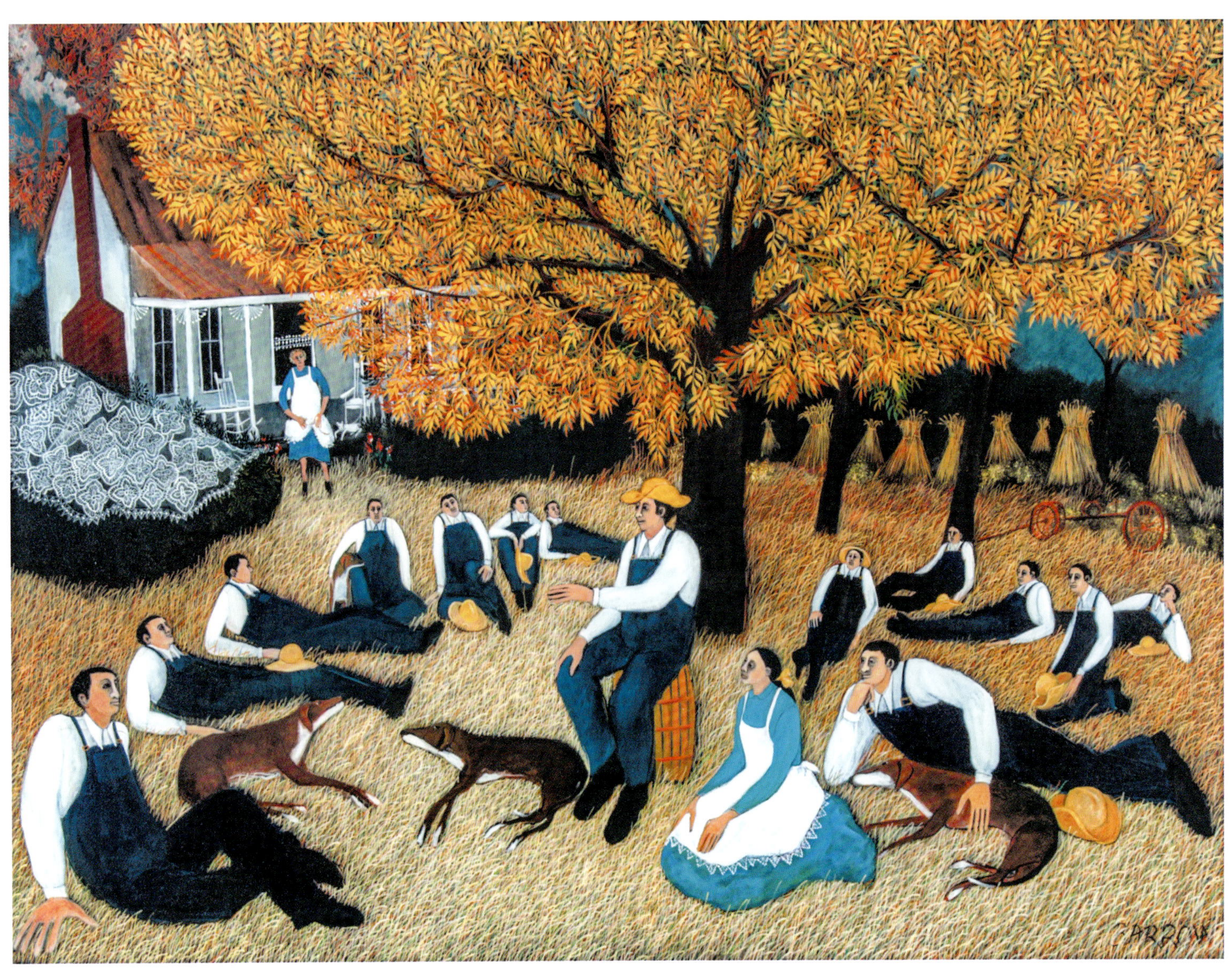

Mary and Martha, 1986, oil on canvas, 30 × 40 inches. Private collection.

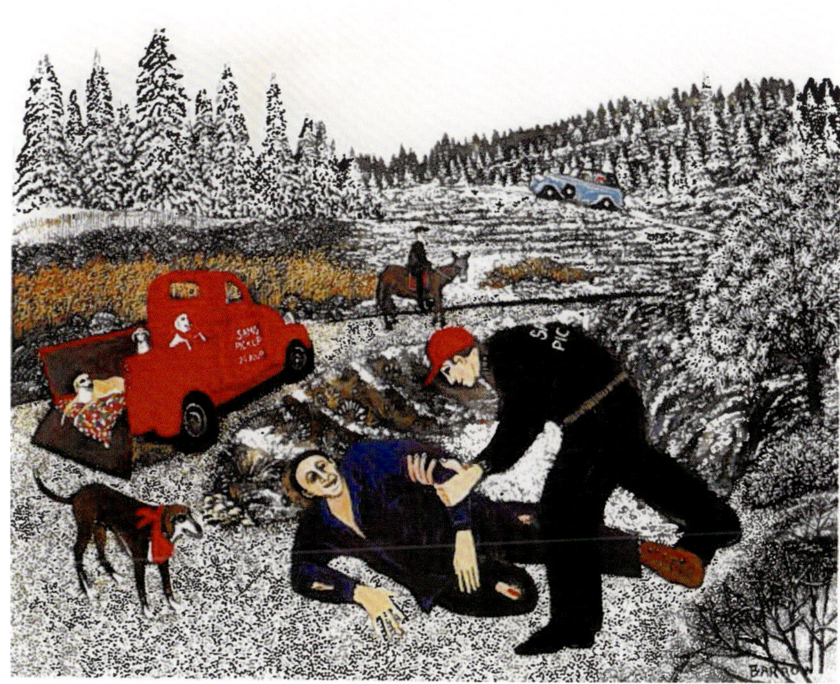

The Good Samaritan #2, 1995, oil on canvas, 24 × 30 inches. Private collection.

Barrow's paintings told us where she traveled, whether it was Turkey, Egypt and the Middle East, England, Spain, or Mexico. Cappadocia in Turkey was probably her most memorable destination. Her Modernist home on Cat Mountain in Austin was a neutral backdrop to the color and pattern of her beloved Mexican folk art and Asian rugs. The rich patterns and color of Turkish rugs and rug shops, lace markets, and produce stands came from her travels. When she traveled with her husband, David, she always wanted to rent a car and stop often to talk to people.

Her figures were more country folk. "Plain people have more pattern in their lives," Barrow once noted. We see them barn dancing or dancing in a procession, courting, shopping, laughing, singing, sewing, conversing with each other, with children running in the rain or catching fireflies. Her paintings are alive with movement, and not just that of her human figures: dogs dash about with kerchiefs tied around their necks, chickens wander, and other animals—cows, sheep, goats—appear as needed to tell a story.

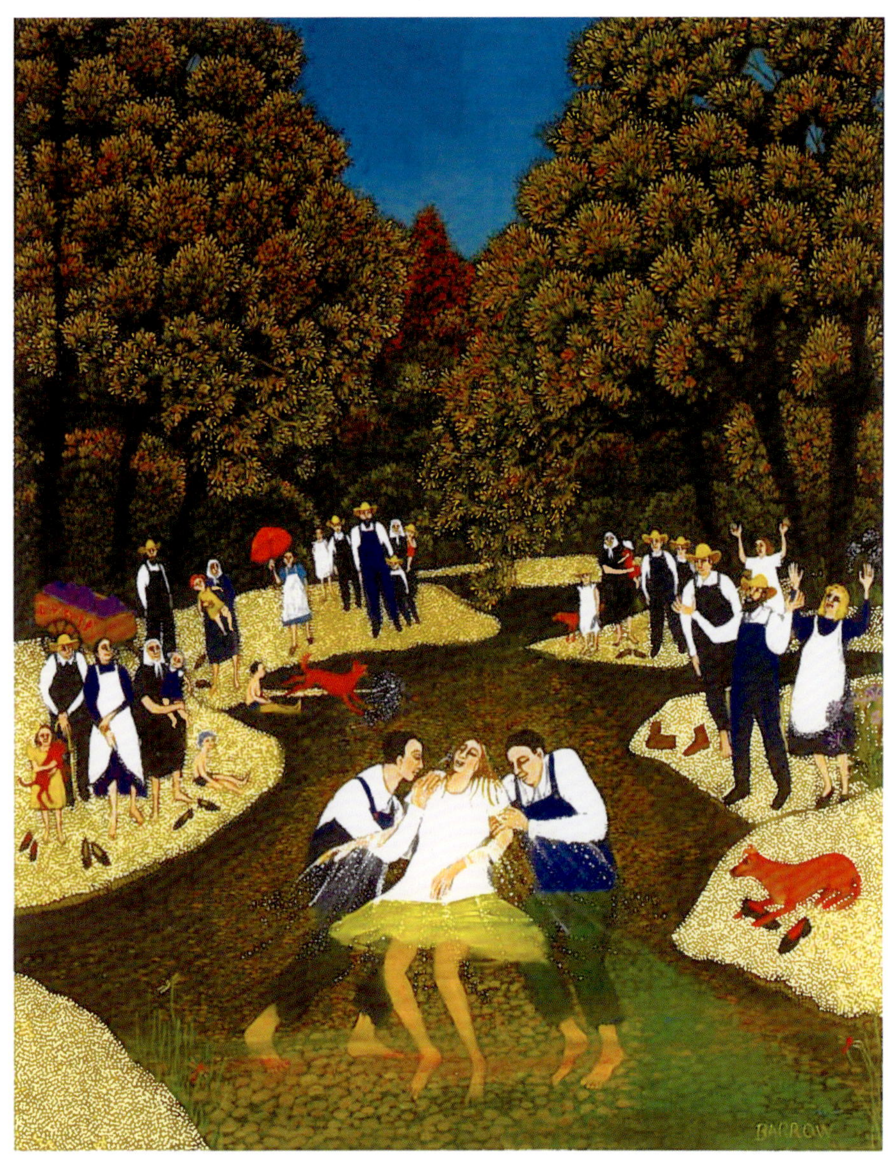

The Baptism of Lydia, 1999, oil on canvas, 30 × 24 inches. Private collection.

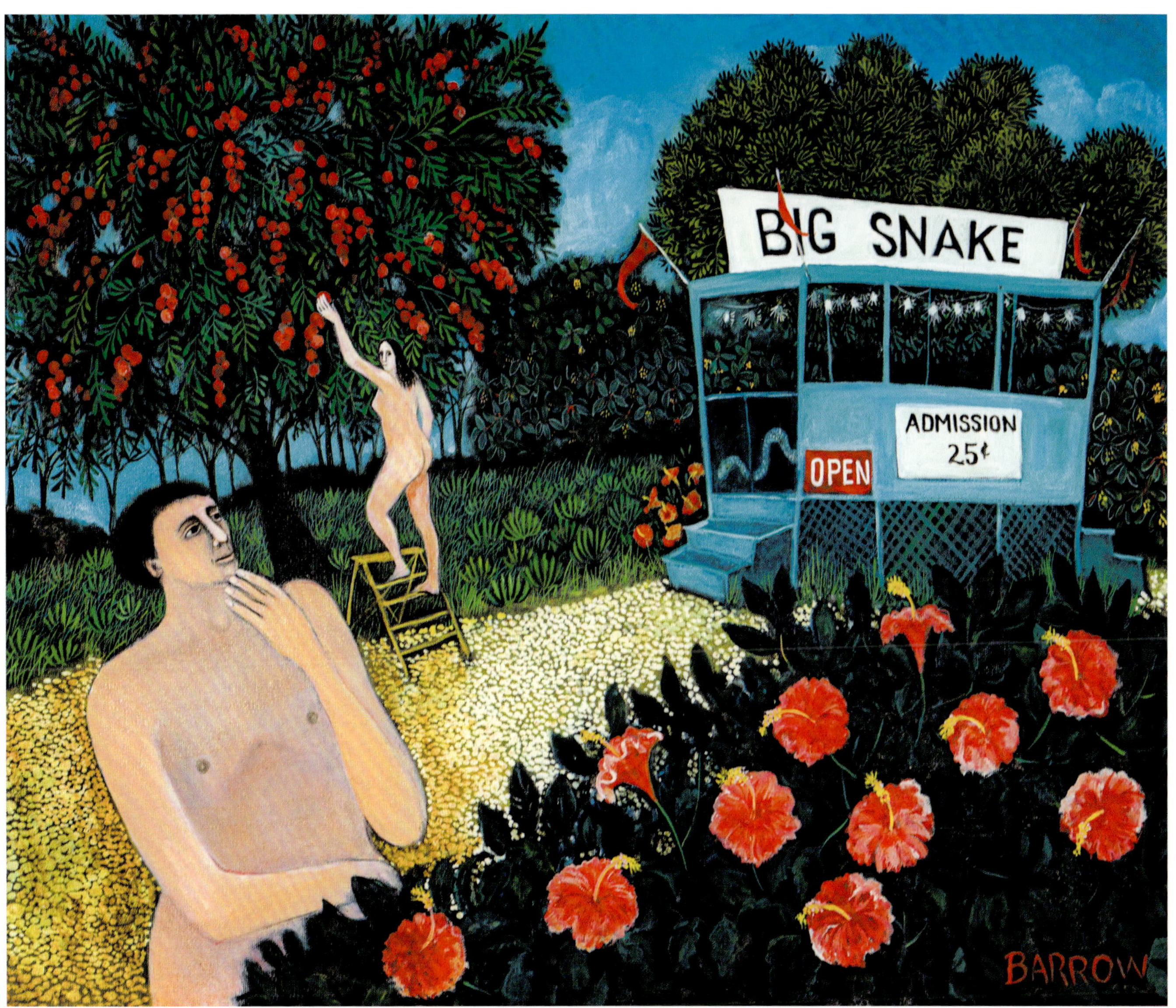

Big Snake, 1989, oil on canvas, 20 × 24 inches. Collection of David Barrow.

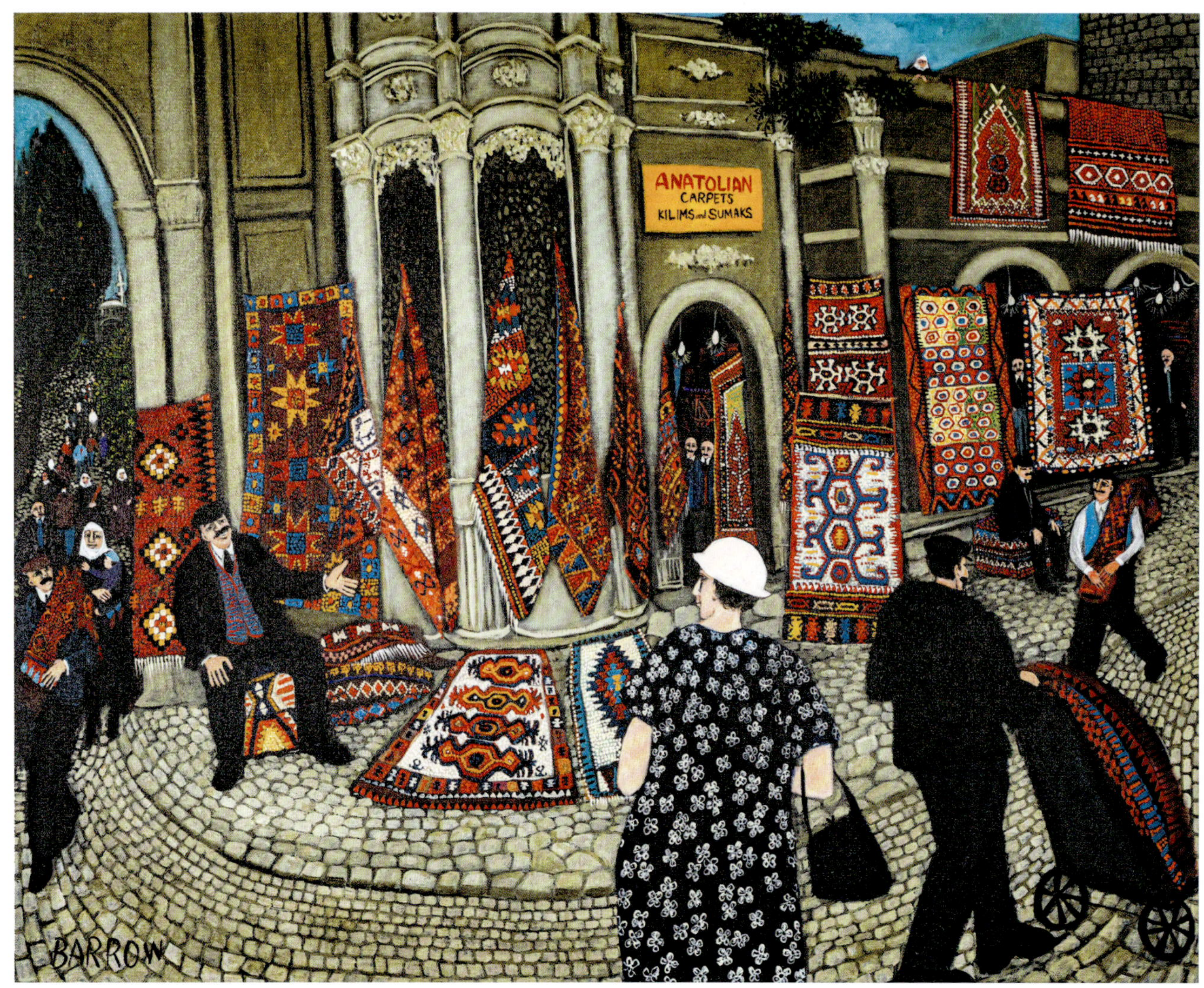

Pretty Lady, Buy a Carpet?, 1999, oil on canvas, 24 × 30 inches. Private collection.

Lu Ann created her joy. When she was a child, family life was not celebratory. She was an only child and envied her friends' extended family events. All her life she admired the warm family life and spiritual core of extended Black families. For her family and supper club evenings, she staged elaborate vignettes in her dining room, some fabricated with papier-mâché sculptures.

Her paintings "cooked," to use Lu Ann's word, for quite a while before she could see all the elements of the compositions in her mind's eye. This planning stage could last for up to four years. The title came early in the process. Then she would search for the parts to convey the story, even taking a road trip around Texas with David to find the right architecture or building to set the figures against (as a background for the action of her subject).

Barrow's folkloric style had matured by the time we began exhibiting her work in Dallas. The elongated necks of her early figures were no longer exaggerated. The color was brighter and applied on a dark background, with thick dots for a gravelly ground or dashes for grassy areas. Every leaf of foliage was delineated and often painted with a translucency that revealed what was behind it. She didn't relate to a straight landscape and needed people and animals to tell the story. There were no shadows cast in her personal perspective.

Pattern is plentiful in a Barrow painting: quilts on clotheslines at a roadside stand, checked shirts, boldly patterned floral dresses with matching shoes, lace-edged tablecloths on the grass bleaching in the sun, Asian rugs, a tie shop offering *Something Different.* Balls on chenille throws, braided rag rugs, and repetitious patterns on wallpaper. One dress fabric recurred in many paintings, a "Jesus face" pattern on a blue ground that Lu Ann saw a Nigerian pilgrim wearing on a trip to the Holy Land with her father in 1983. She re-created the image from memory when her camera malfunctioned.

Generations appear in a haberdashery in *A Family Business,* or in three generations admiring the windows of a bridal shop in *Past, Present, Future,* or in the families arriving in their trucks for Christmas at the snow-covered country home of grandparents whose arms are outstretched in welcome.

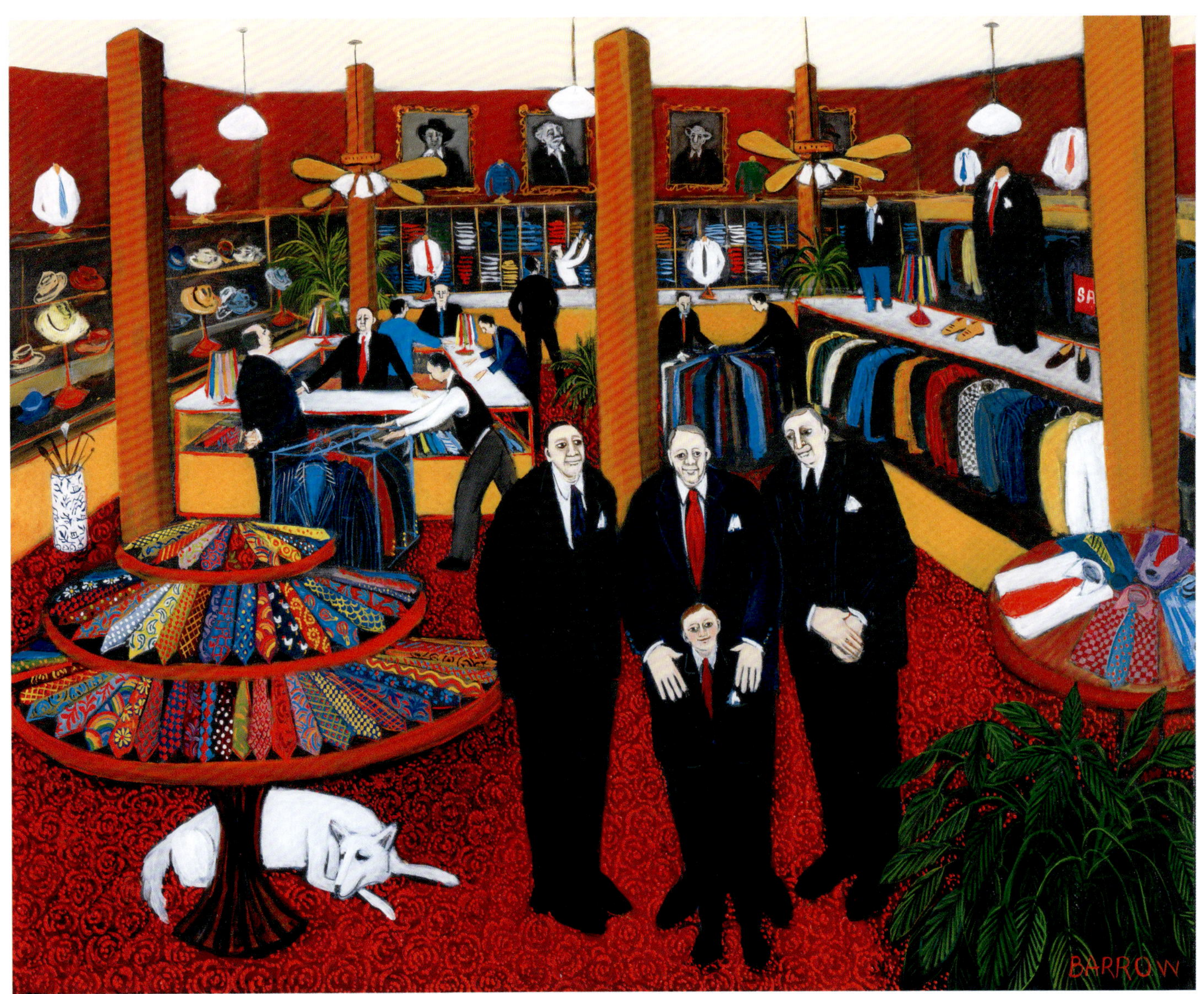

A Family Business, 2001, oil on canvas, 24 × 30 inches. Private collection.

Lu Ann loved to read and suggested many great books that I have enjoyed. The first was *The Bear Went over the Mountain* by William Kotzwinkle. I stopped everything to read a book that Lu Ann suggested and even compiled a list of the books, fiction and nonfiction, she reveled in. I have shared the list with many of her fans. Lu Ann's own reading would generate ideas for paintings on occasion. Learning about the 1856 acquisition of camels by the US Army Camel Corps, a little-known element of Texas history, led to a large painting, *Camel Days in Texas*.

In 1999, the Texas Book Festival reproduced Lu Ann's *Bluebonnet Belles* on posters, T-shirts, and mugs. They had to be reprinted twice because of their popularity and were sold out yet again. Subsequently, she was commissioned to paint *Book Lovers*, which was reproduced on the inaugural National Book Festival poster in 2001.

The holidays of Christmas, Easter, Day of the Dead, and July Fourth weren't the only celebratory subjects. James Housefield sums it up: "Barrow's painted world embodies joy. Filled with laughter and friendship, it is a world in which the patterns of everyday life are cause enough for celebration."

There is laughter when friends gather, whether two leaning in on a settee for gossip or a good joke, or for Lu Ann's own high school class reunion, *You Haven't Changed a Bit*, which was delayed while the organizers tried to lose weight. Beauty parlors with patterned walls, floral dresses, and lace curtains set the stage of camaraderie around the hair dryers *Inside Donna's Hair* and in *Barber Shop Humor*, where the men lined up are all laughing. Events outside a feed store in *Chicken Jokes and Big Reds* have hilarious results for the four men set among their trucks loaded with chickens, the ever-present dogs, and bluebonnets and Indian paintbrush blooming in the foreground.

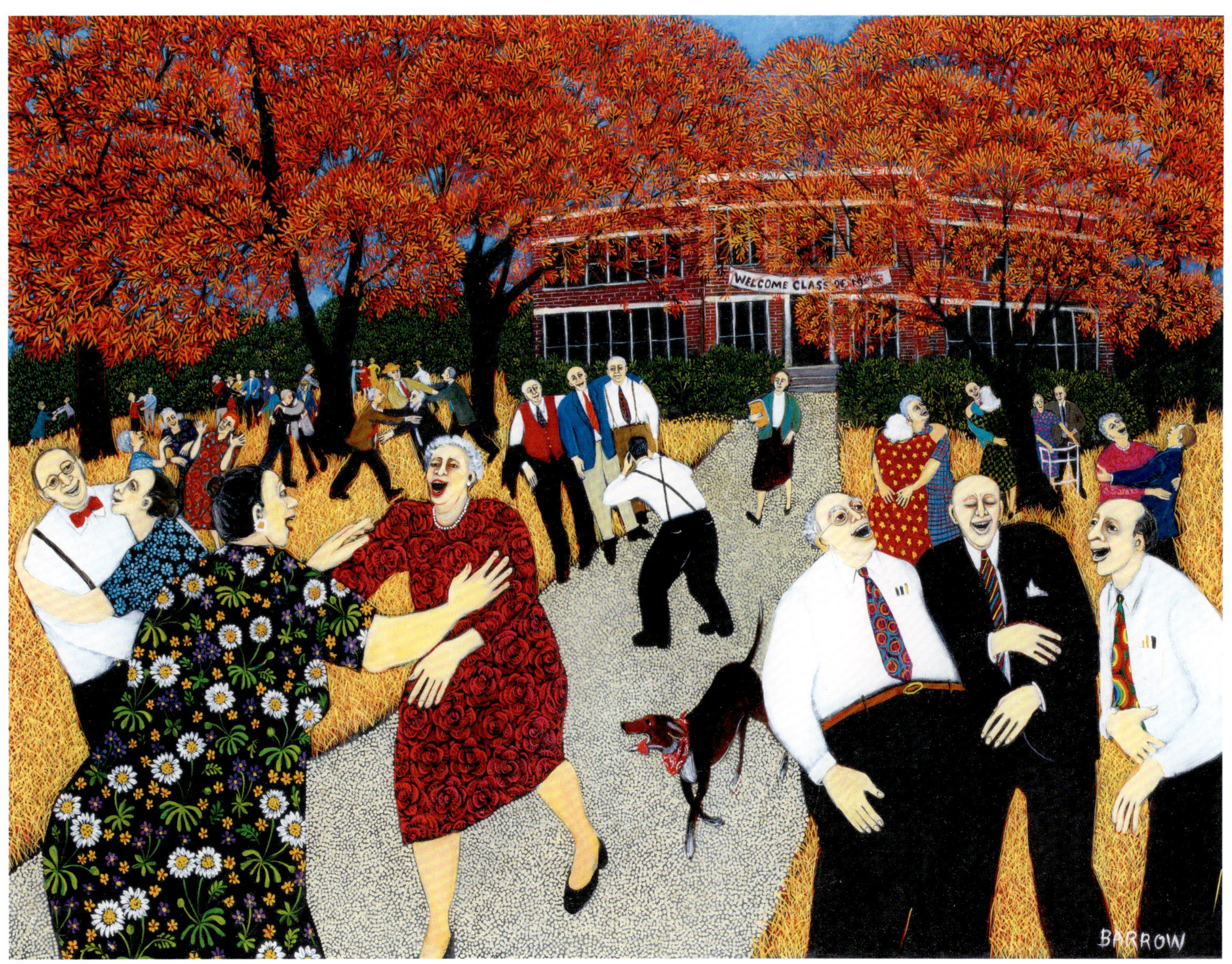

You Haven't Changed a Bit, 1997, oil on canvas, 30 × 40 inches. Private collection.

In 2006 we collected eighty-five paintings from their generous owners to create two simultaneous exhibitions at the Austin Museum of Art and the Longview Museum of Fine Arts. A forty-page catalog gave an overview of the paintings in both exhibitions, and Lu Ann contributed comments about the paintings throughout the catalog. After these two exhibitions, we planned a retrospective exhibition at Valley House before we returned the assembled paintings. It was a huge effort to pick up all the paintings and assemble the catalog, but one I am proud of.

Valley House had a long list of Barrow fans who wanted to be called when new work arrived. Her unique style of narrative paintings captivated our audience as well as a few well-known personalities when we exhibited them outside the gallery at art fairs in New York, Philadelphia, Atlanta, and Dallas.

The last paintings we offered were painted in 2010. After that time Lu Ann was plagued by health challenges but always hoped she could walk up the stairs to her studio loft over the kitchen again. She continued to plan compositions in her mind and tell me about them in our phone conversations. It was a great privilege to expand awareness of Lu Ann Barrow's paintings beyond her hometown of Austin and especially to know her as a friend.

A testament to the enduring quality of Lu Ann Barrow's paintings is that very few have come back to us since we sold the first paintings in 1992; they have become part of the fabric of family life for those lucky enough to live with them.

LU ANN BARROW'S PAINTINGS OF IMAGINATION AND EXPERIENCE

James Housefield

Lu Ann Barrow paints a magical world. Though not a world that most of us inhabit, Barrow's world seems comfortingly familiar. Located somewhere not far from here, in a not-so-distant past, her works are populated by figures from her imagination. Barrow studied art at the University of Texas at Austin from 1952 through 1956, when abstract painting dominated the art world. Since her student days she has chosen to work outside of the language of abstract art, instead inserting abstract forms into the figurative scenes she imagines. Deep historical traditions enrich her distinct pictorial sensibilities and folkloric style. Rich textures and patterns within Barrow's compositions evoke Persian, Indian, and Medieval European illuminated manuscripts as well as the modern art of Pierre Bonnard and Henri Matisse. Barrow has long found inspiration in the work of Vincent van Gogh and the Impressionists. Her approach is more closely aligned with that of their lesser-known contemporary Henri Rousseau. Celebrated by modern artists from Pablo Picasso to the Surrealists, Rousseau inspired many to paint with an "innocent eye" as if they were untrained or naïve artists. Barrow's art thus engages modern traditions of willful "primitivism" stemming from Rousseau that recur throughout twentieth-century art, from Marc Chagall to Jean Dubuffet to David Bates. Barrow, Austin's heir to Rousseau, is a visual storyteller.

Barrow's painted world embodies joy. Filled with laughter and friendship, it is a world in which the patterns of everyday life are cause enough for celebration. "I can't do a painting that's not celebratory," Barrow says with a smile. Groups of people fill her paintings, yet the rare solitary figure she paints is never truly alone. For instance, the woman lost in songful delight shares her joy with the orange cat upon her lap as she accompanies *The Gospel Hour* on her radio. Alone except for the animals around them, the gardener absorbed in trimming *Photinia* and the knitter engaged in *Ozark Industry* find pleasure in their activities that echoes Barrow's own delight in painting. Happy reverie fills the expression of a woman in pearly white dress who, with her dog, sits surrounded by other shoppers as she awaits the man trying on *The White Suit*. In groups, as with the women who work together in *The Pattern*, the sense of joy expands as it becomes increasingly social. A love of their work and the relationships with people and animals around them give them cause for celebration. Everyday activities like sewing, shopping, talking, and gardening contain their own purpose, satisfaction, and joy in Barrow's world.

Celebration infuses her figures' expressions, gestures, and characters, as well as the landscapes and architectural elements Barrow creates. In *Barn Dance*, for instance, a repetition of roof beams calls attention to the dancers' repeated forms below. A string of lights seems to dance as it wraps its way across the rafters and thus across the composition. A rainbow backdrop behind the three-piece band inverts the arcs of tricolor fabric that decorate the scene. Quilts, central features of so many of Barrow's paintings, hang high in the barn, their playful patterns seemingly as mobile as the patterned dresses on the dance floor below. Although her painting techniques are as guided by intuition as they are by planning, Barrow's empathy for her subjects and her eye for animated design fill this world with joyous movement.

On a formal level, the repeated patterns that permeate her compositions animate the paintings visually and psychologically. Morning glory flowers explode across the landscape behind the gathering of *Brothers, Sisters, Mothers, and Others*. Those same flowers animate the jubilant dresses of two girls and a woman from their group. In *Rainy Night*, raindrops look almost like Morse code messages of dots and dashes descending from the skies. Barrow's painting begins from an observation of nature's patterns (picture a flash photograph taken on a rainy evening). She then creates drama from the designs that result as the rain rakes across the scene. Whether formal or social, these patterns instill deep and intriguing textures that energize Barrow's compositions.

Barrow's poetic narratives, like those of Rousseau, emerge from a convergence of careful observation, lived experience, and vivid imagination. Childhood memories from the small community of Rosenberg, Texas, surface in her art from time to time; East Texas pine forests reappear in many paintings. Unlike Rousseau (who never strayed far from his Paris home), Barrow has traveled extensively and enriched her art through these voyages. Though its horsedrawn carriages would be at home in a Rousseau painting, *Invitation to Tea* was inspired by her repeated visits to Egypt beginning in 1976. Whereas travel snapshots inspired its painted architecture and camels, the larger story of *Invitation to Tea* emerged from the artist's mind. Memory and imagination, together, create the vibrant spaces of her world. Barrow's working methods range from careful study to imaginative creation. "The things that I paint are what I've lived, and read, or things that come to me in the night," she explains. She often begins painting without sketching any preliminary composition, allowing figures to enter the scene as if they were living characters responding to the stories that play out as a painting grows. "Words have special meaning; they float to me. I have the title before I paint, because the title nearly always triggers the painting." Once, in an Austin store, she overheard one shopper recall the previous day's activities, proclaiming that they'd had "a hallelujah time." The resulting painting, *Hallelujah Time*, envisions that celebration as if it were a parallel to a New Orleans jazz funeral, complete with trumpet and ornate umbrellas, set in a piney Texas woods.

Similarly, *Soul-Journers* takes its title from a word coined by a travel guide she met when visiting Cana, in Israel, the city whose architecture is recognizable in the painting. "We all are soul-journers," the guide explained. For Barrow, this spoke of a universal and quintessentially human journey confined to no single faith. "Everyone who came to the Holy Land, whether they were Christian, Jew, or Muslim . . . they were all soul-journers." A sojourn is a temporary stay; "soul-journers" metaphorically refers to the soul's brief time on Earth and to a personal spiritual quest. As such, the title addresses the manifold concerns of Barrow's paintings. In Barrow's world, the quest for meaning in life is grounded in everyday activities and relationships, even when that meaning unfolds in religious stories.

A comforting spirituality infuses daily life in Barrow's religious art. She credits a Bible study course in the 1970s as "the catalyst" for an immense body of work. She emphasizes that the Bible scenes "don't look any different from the other paintings. I put Jesus in overalls or regular clothes, and the disciples the same." When she paints the familiar New Testament parable of the Good Samaritan, Barrow sets it in a snowy landscape, and revels in the patterns created by frost and snow upon the roadside, trees, and fields. Travelers (including a clergyman) pass by, leaving an injured man to be rescued by the driver of a red truck filled with happy dogs. His clothing and truck are emblazoned with the motto "SAMS PICKUP 24 HOUR." Like artists of the Renaissance who updated biblical scenes by setting them in contemporary times, Barrow emphasizes the continuing relevance of Old and New Testament stories.

Whether painting biblical scenes, a *Barn Dance*, a gathering of *Brothers, Sisters, Mothers, and Others*, or the infectious laughter of *Barber Shop Humor*, Barrow can count on audiences meeting her halfway and filling in the details of the stories she recounts. For today's viewers, more accustomed to the visual stories of film and video than to those of Renaissance murals or illuminated manuscripts, each of these paintings may recall a scene from a motion picture. Her cinematic moments expand in the imagination, rewarding the journeys of a viewer's creative soul. Lu Ann Barrow's paintings joyfully recount a world in which the simple gatherings of friends and family are inherently a celebration of life.

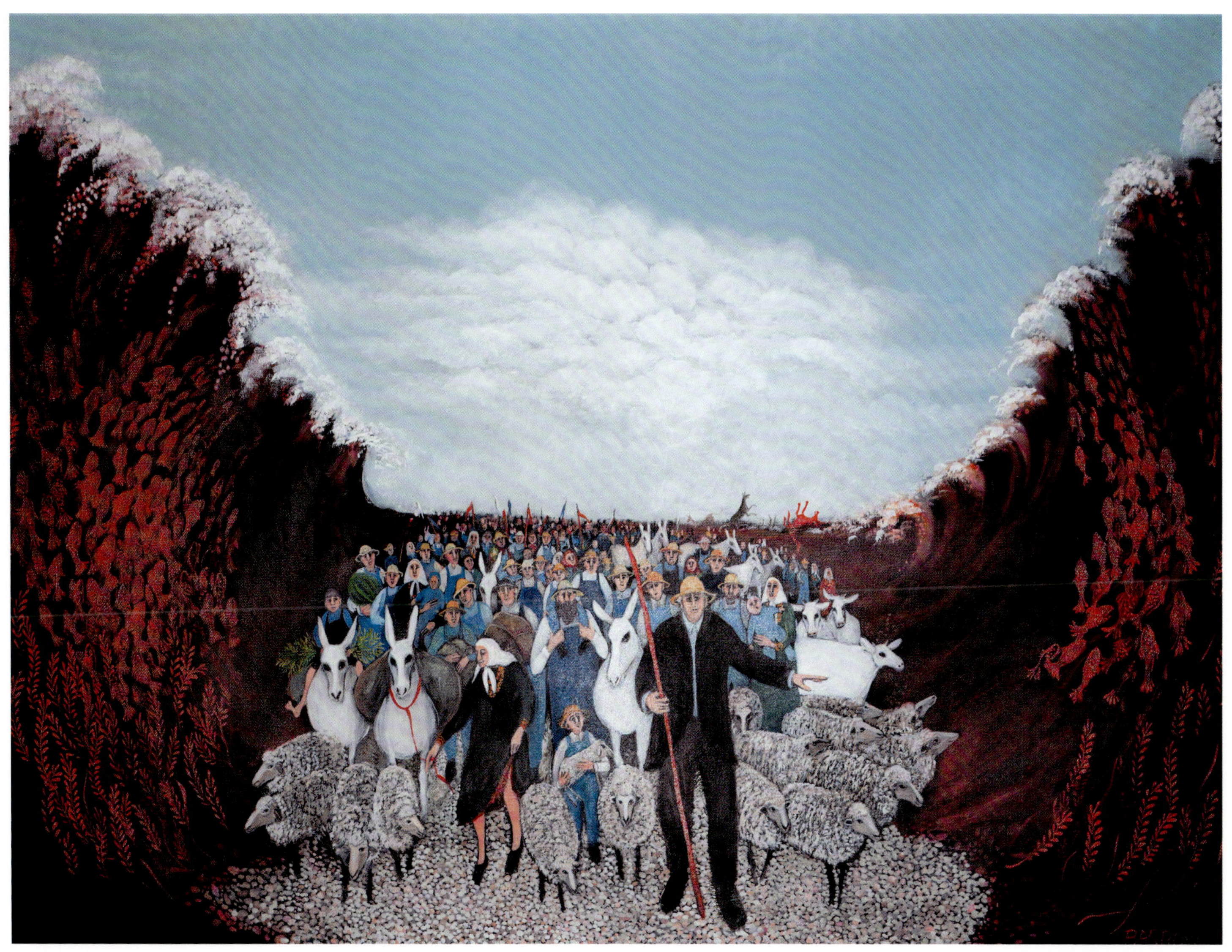

Parting of the Red Sea, n.d., oil on canvas, 25 × 35 inches. Private collection.

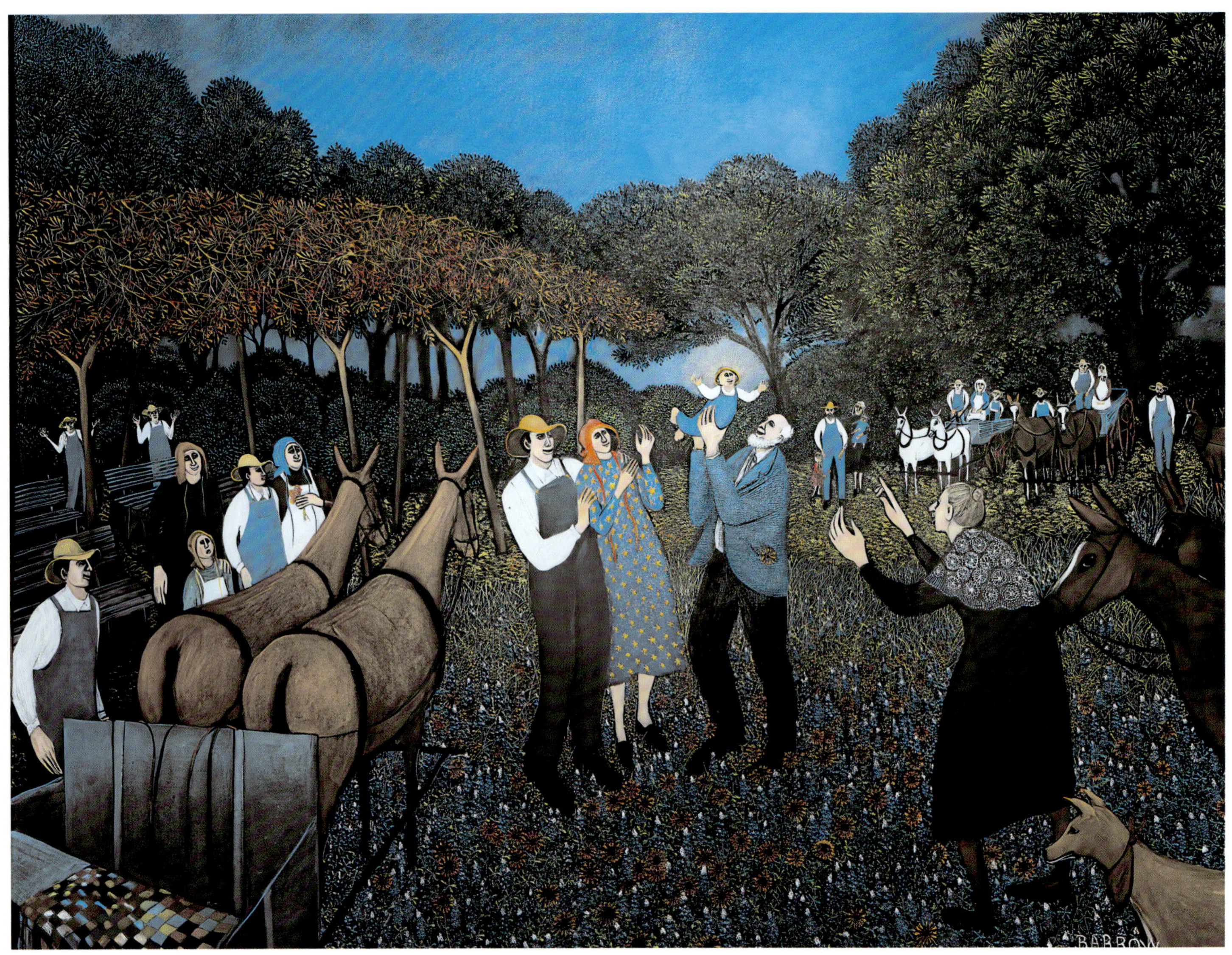

Ain't He a Fine Boy? n.d., oil on canvas, 30 × 40 inches. Private collection.

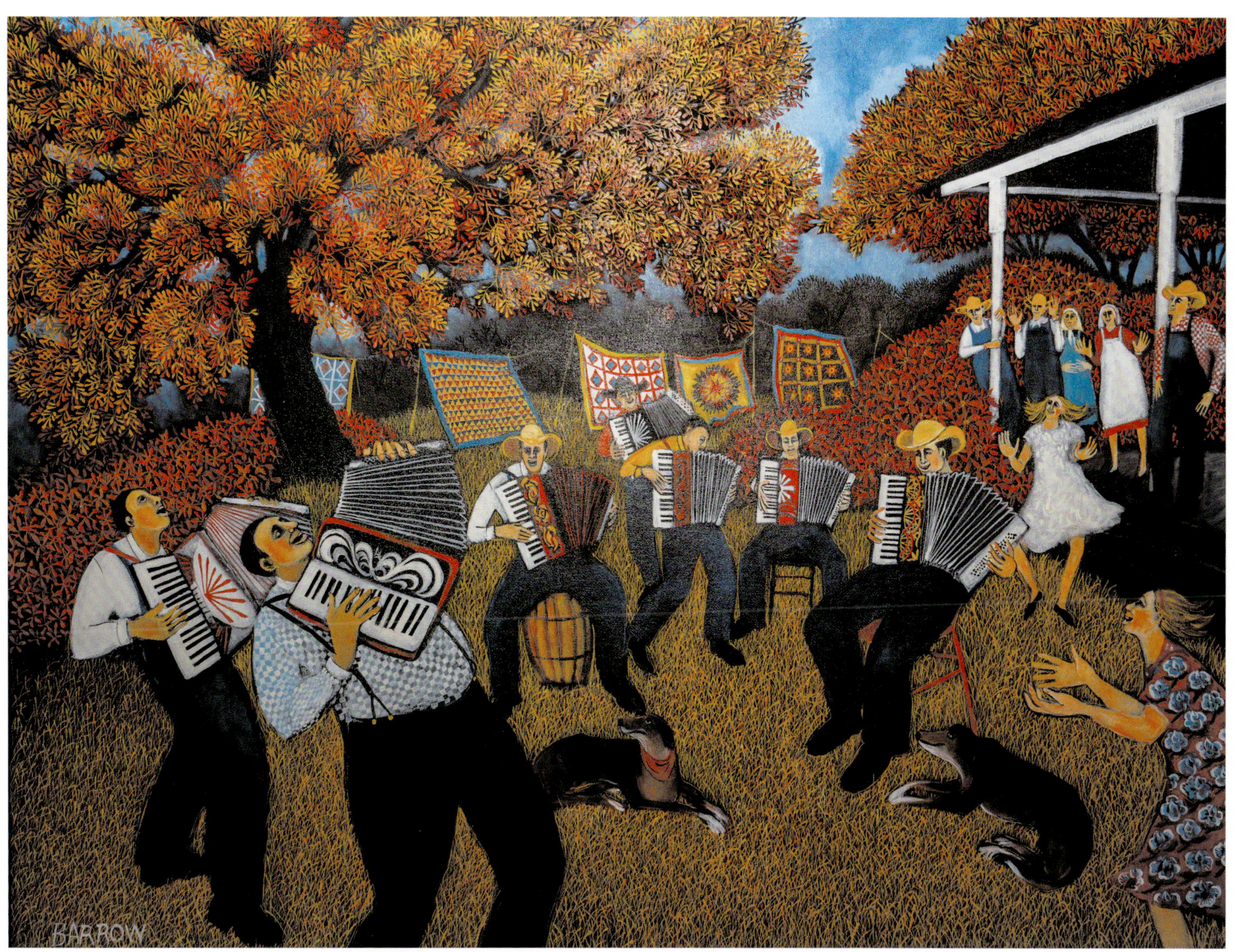

Accordion Kings, n.d., oil on canvas, 30 × 40 inches. Private collection.

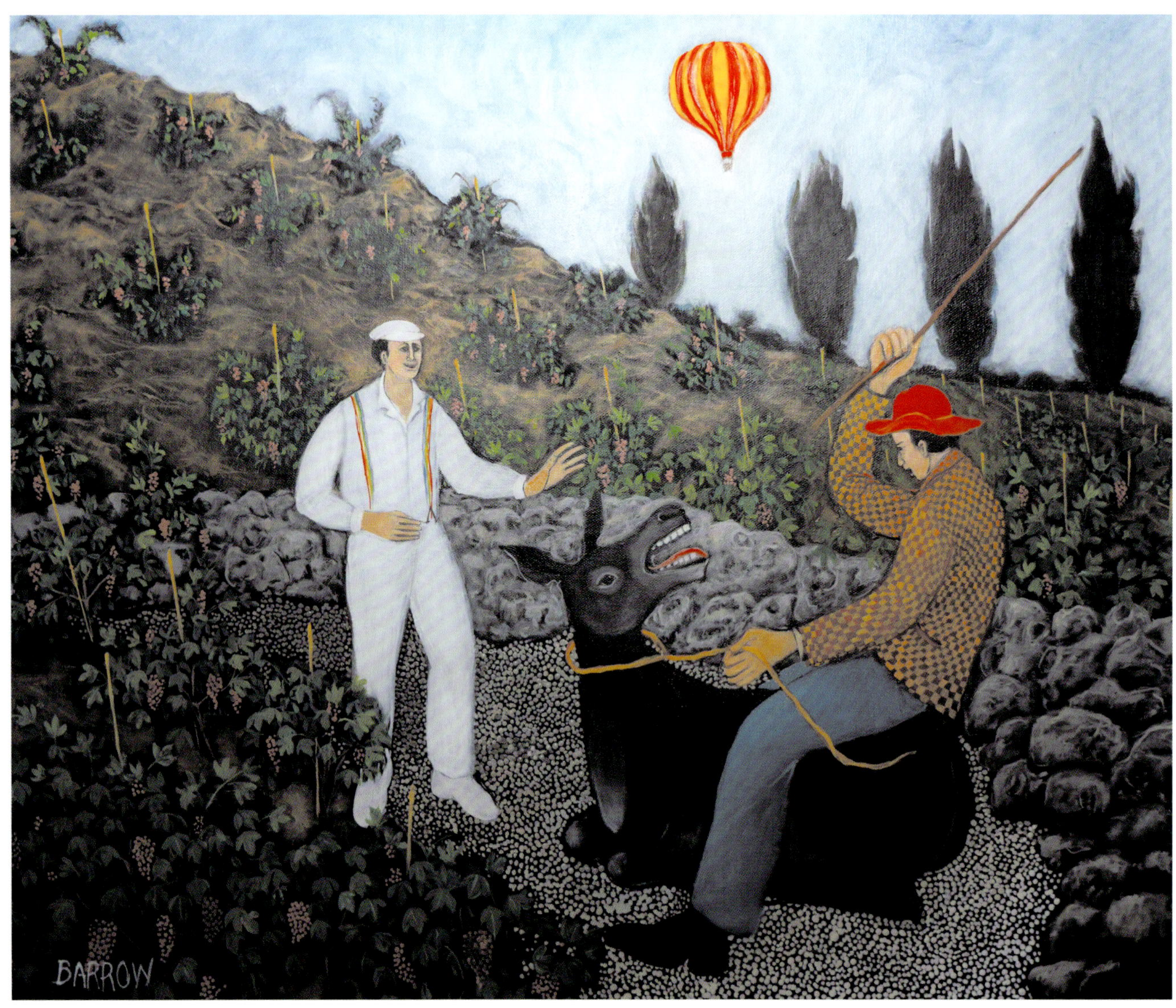

Balaam's Ass, n.d., oil on canvas, 20 × 24 inches. Private collection.

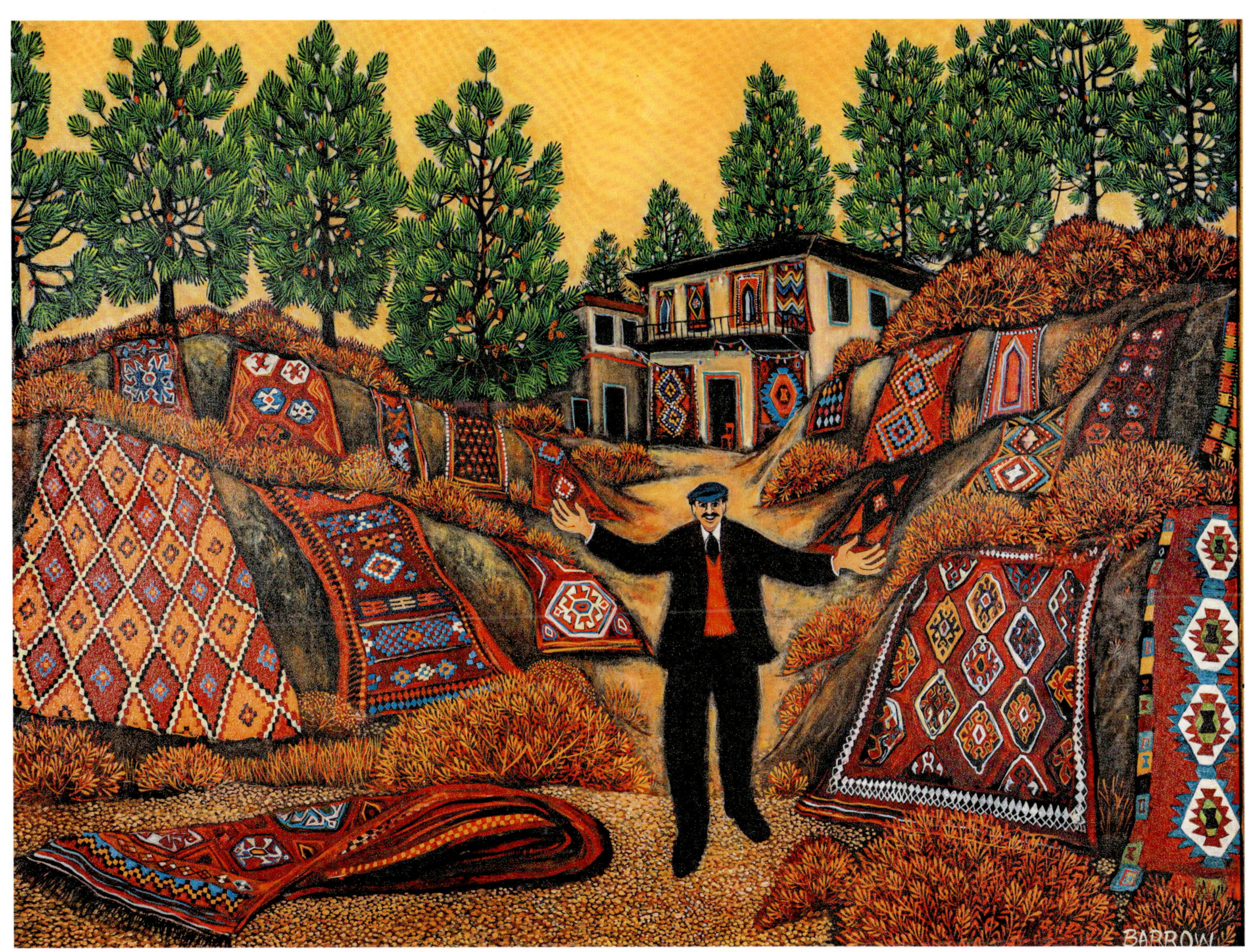

Welcome to My Rugs, n.d., oil on canvas, 40 × 30 inches. Private collection.

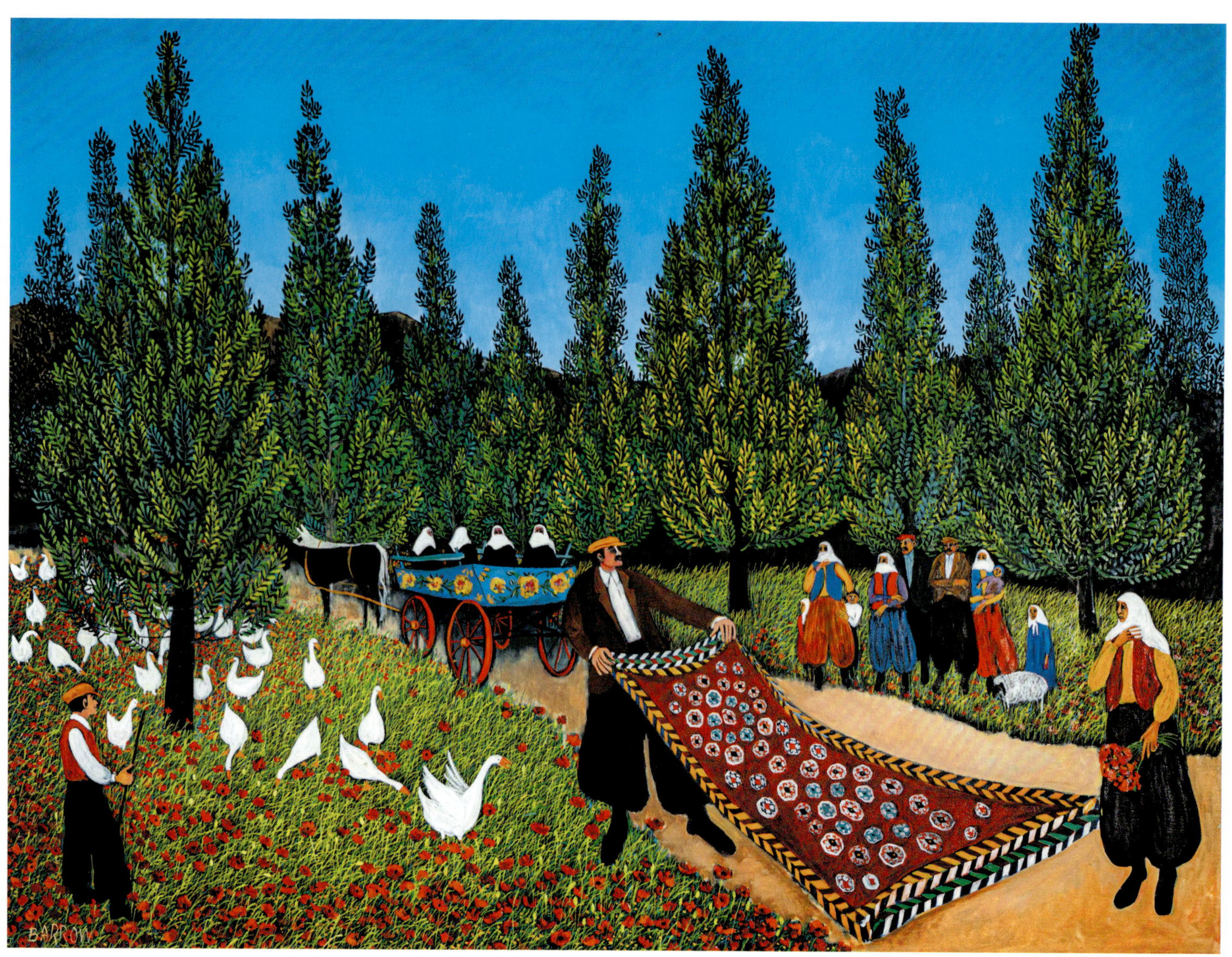

The Turkish Rug Vendor, n.d., oil on canvas, 36 × 48 inches. Private collection.

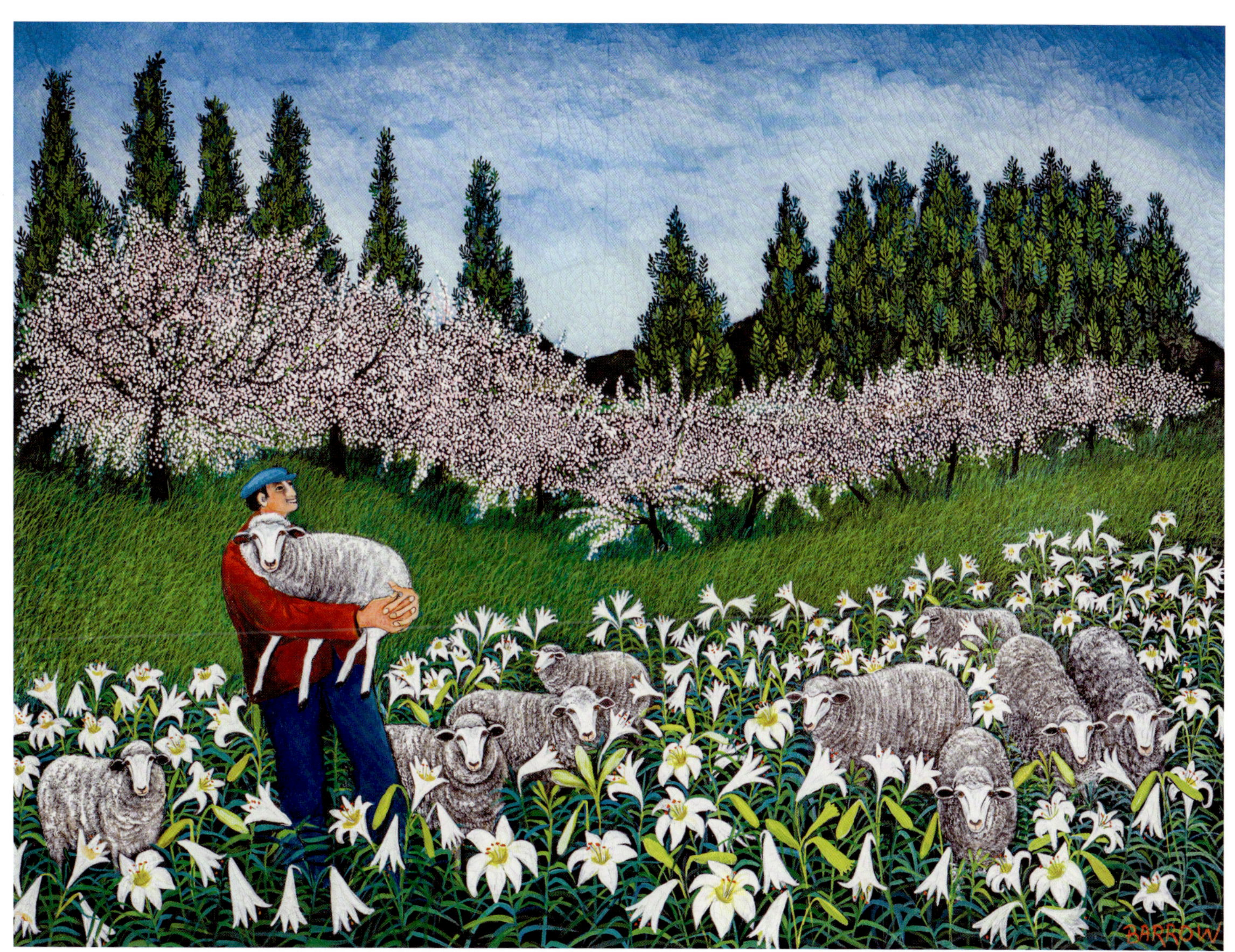

He Pastures His Flock in Fields, n.d., oil on canvas, 36 × 40 inches. Collection of David Barrow.

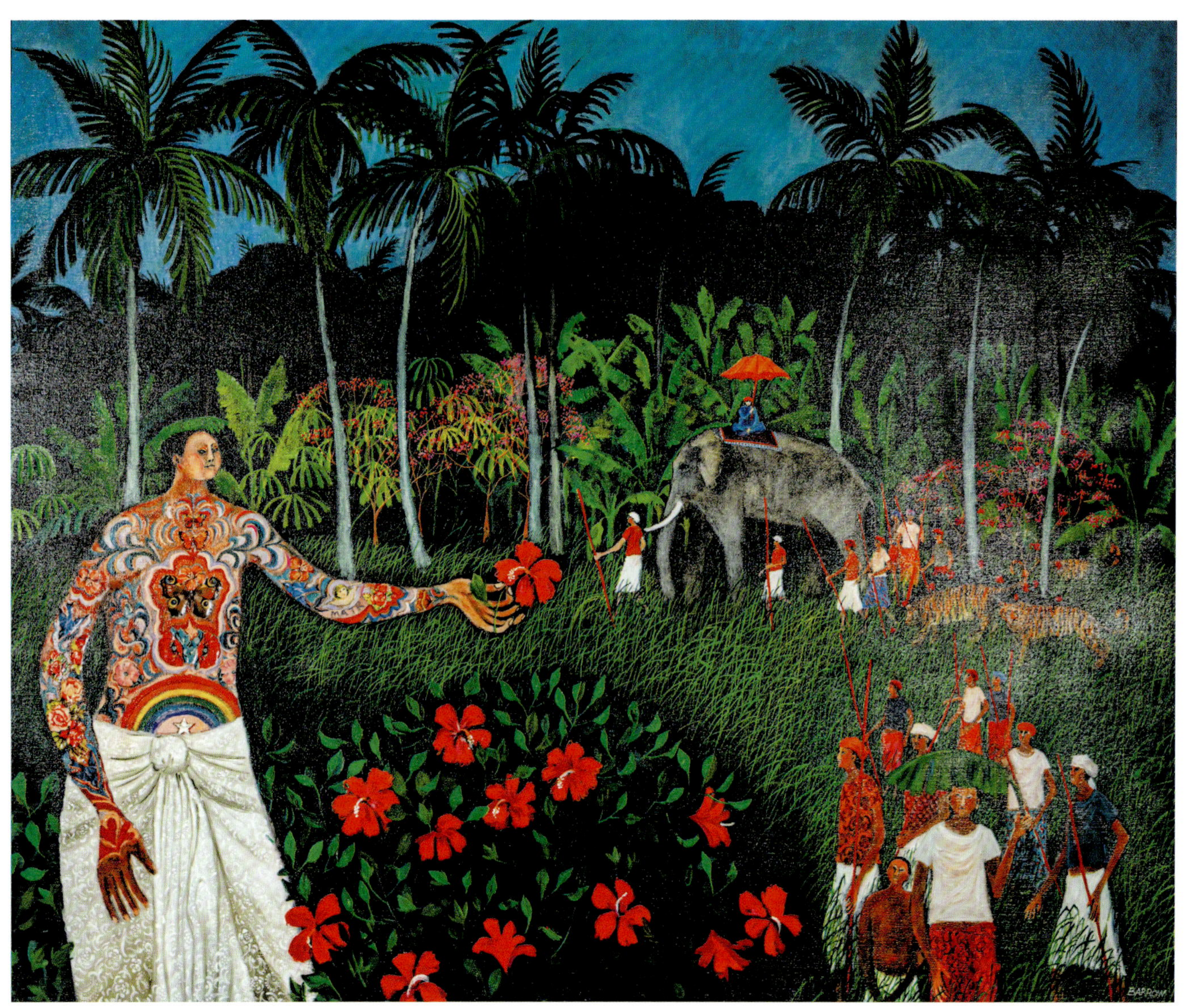

Marco Polo and the Tattoo Man, n.d., oil on canvas, 49 × 40½ inches. Private collection.

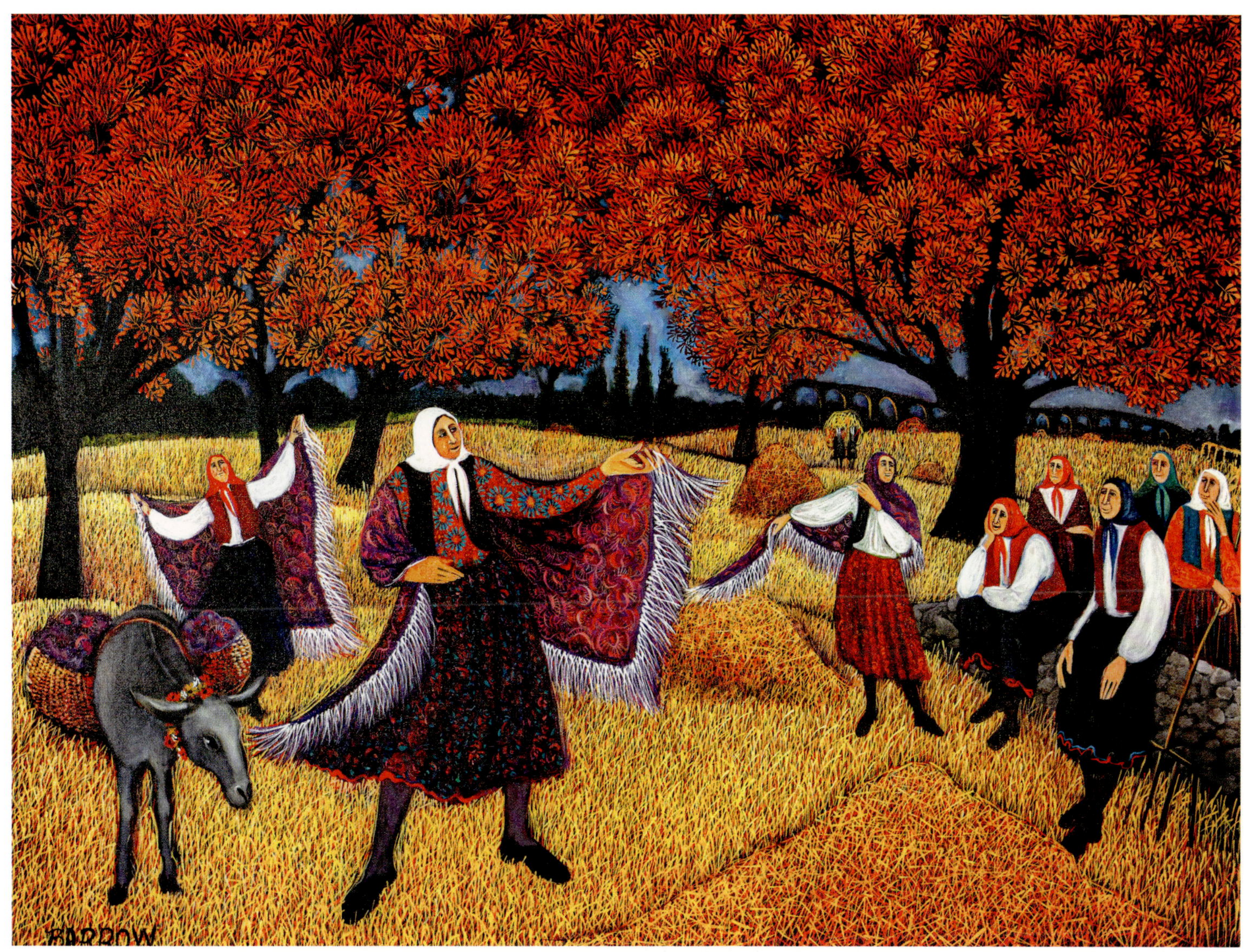

Lydia, Seller of Purple Goods, n.d., oil on canvas, 43 × 33 inches. Private collection.

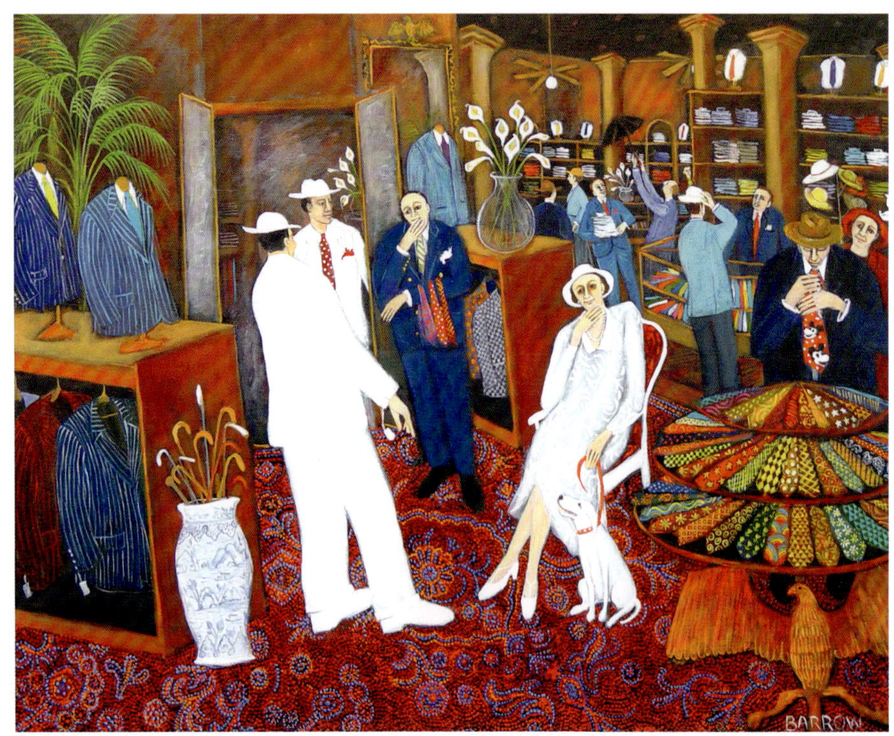

The White Suit, n.d., oil on canvas, 24 × 30 inches. Private collection.

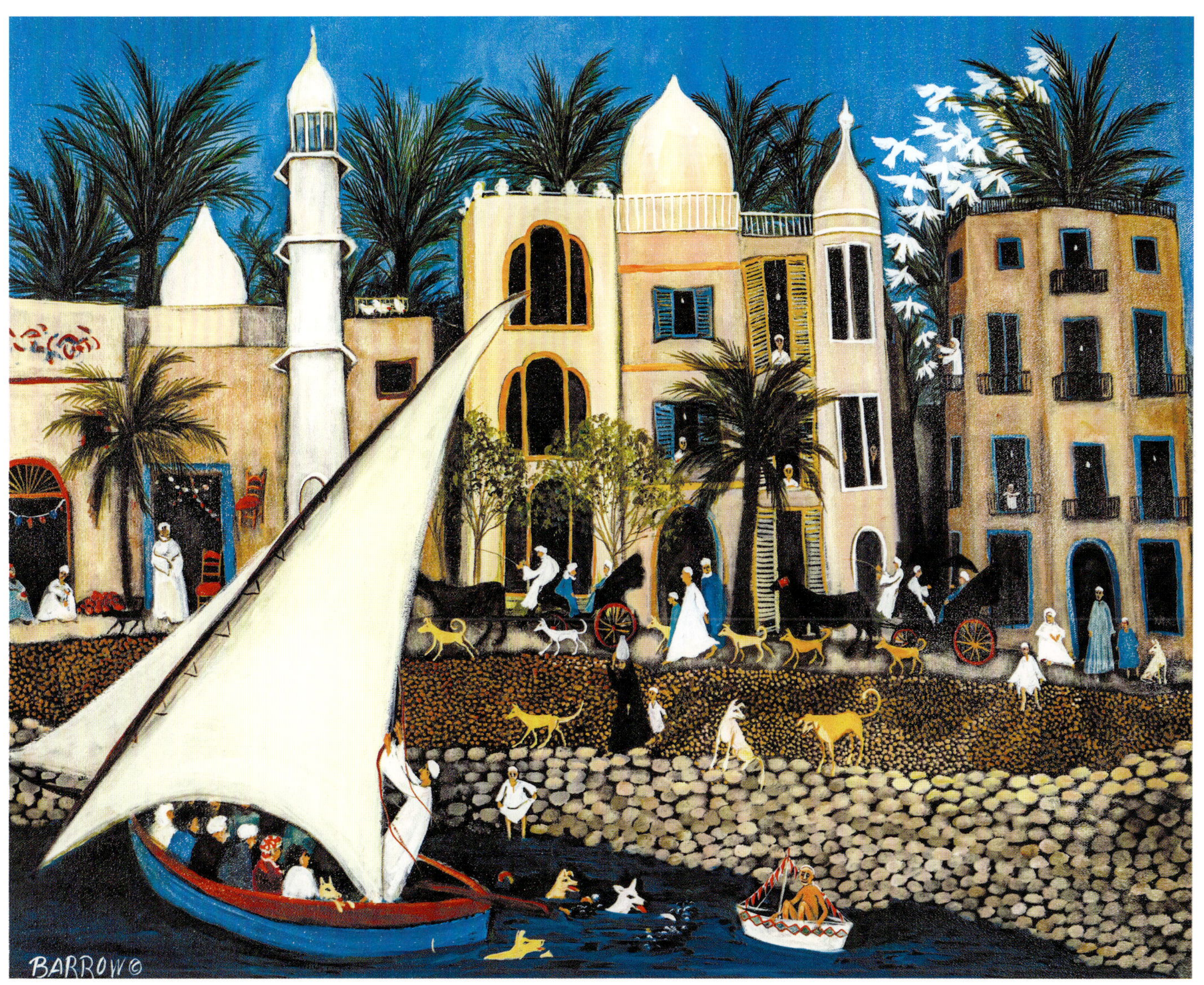

Sailboat, n.d., oil on canvas, 23 × 28 inches. Collection of David Barrow.

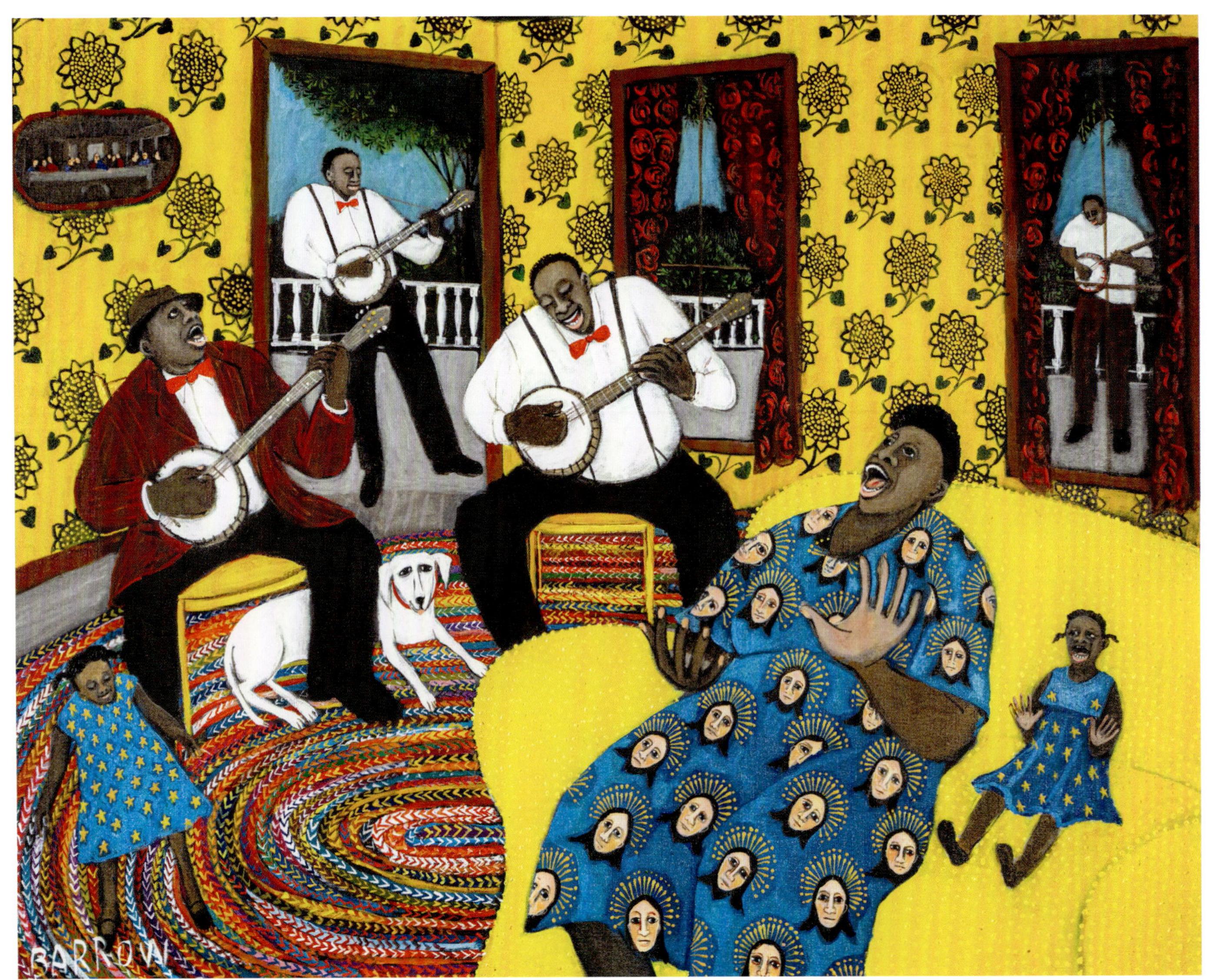

Banjo Brothers, 2001, oil on canvas, 24 × 30 inches. Private collection.

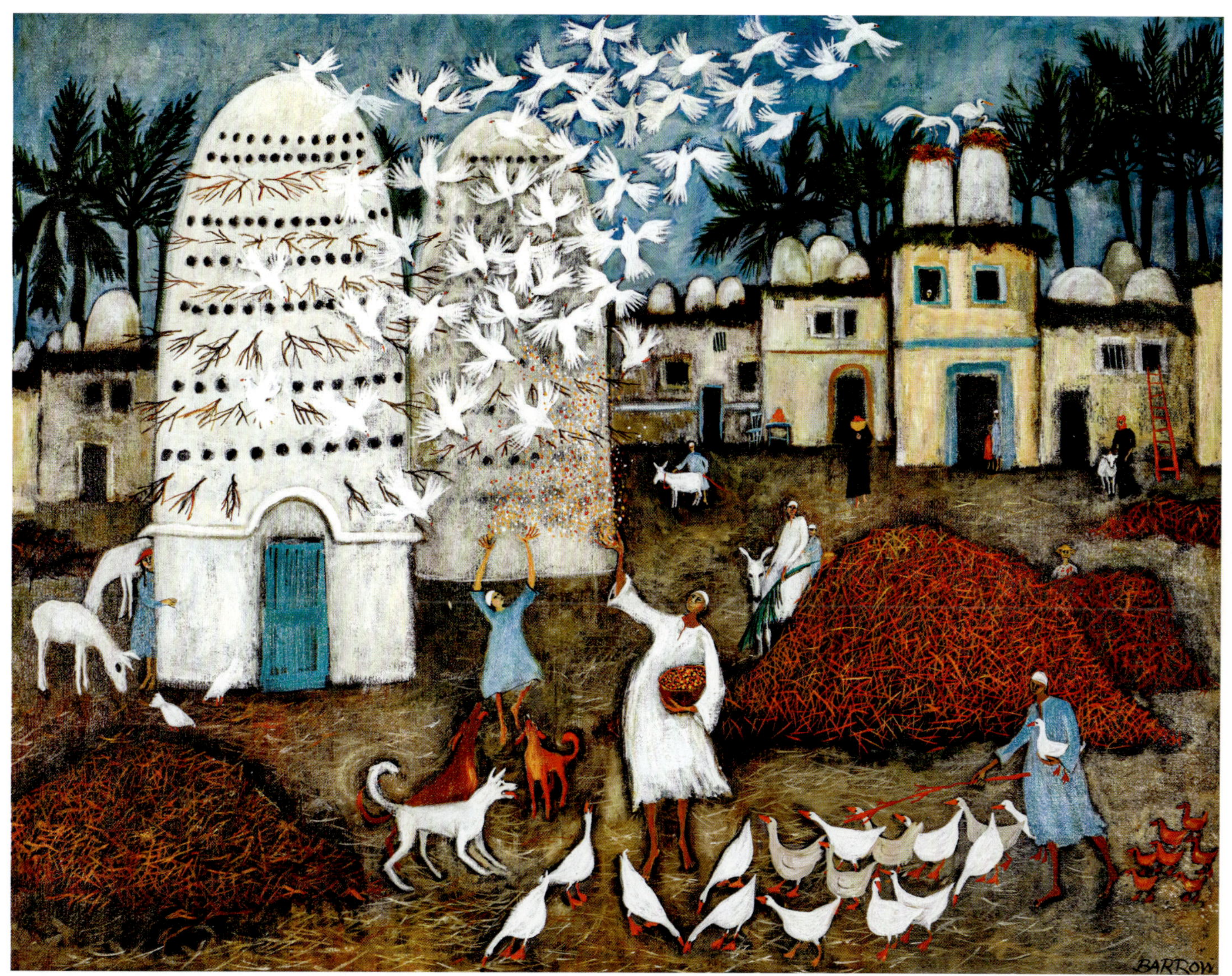

The Pigeon Feeders, n.d., oil on canvas, 28 × 36 inches. Collection of David Barrow.

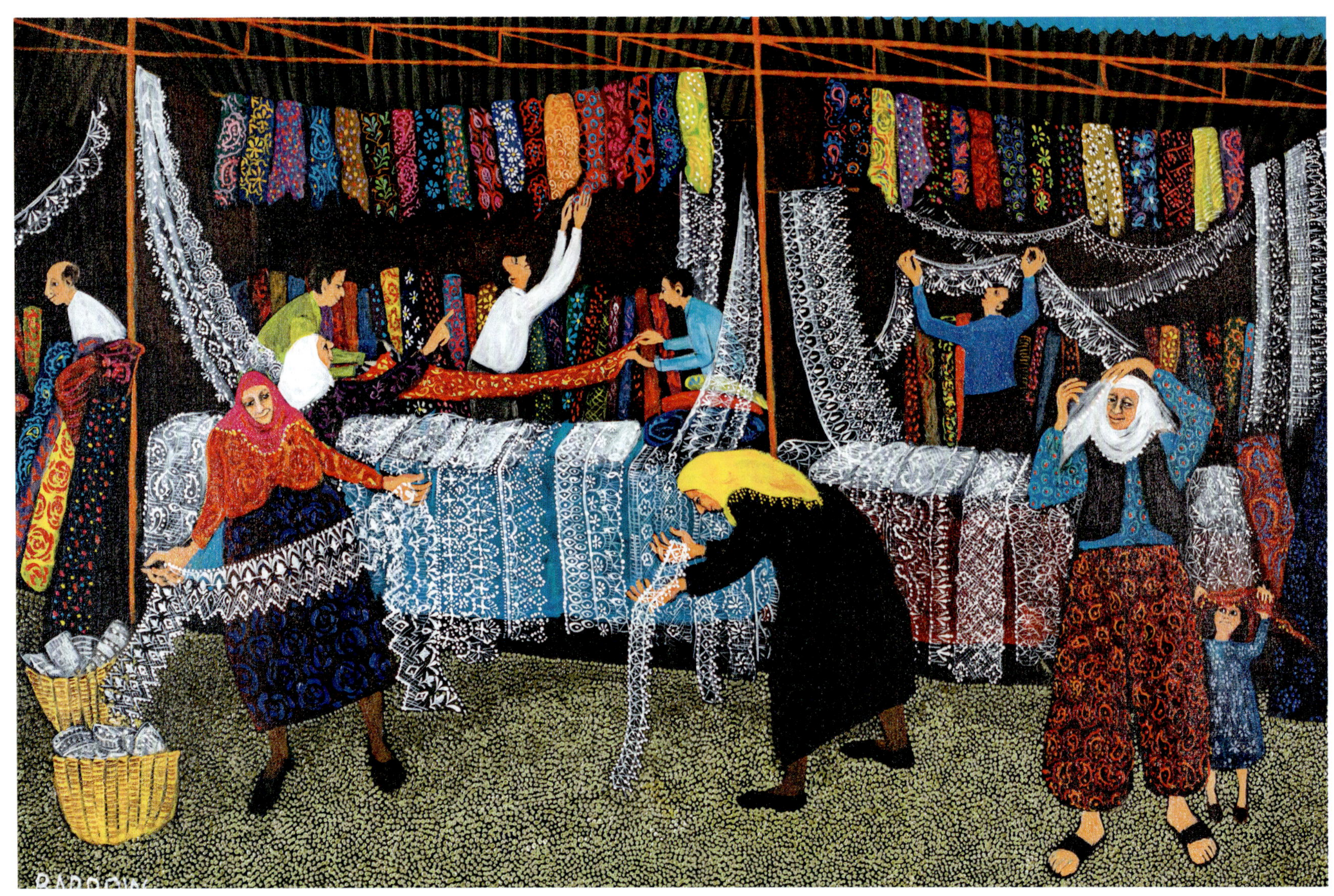

A Little Bit of Lace, n.d., oil on canvas, 20 × 30 inches. Private collection.

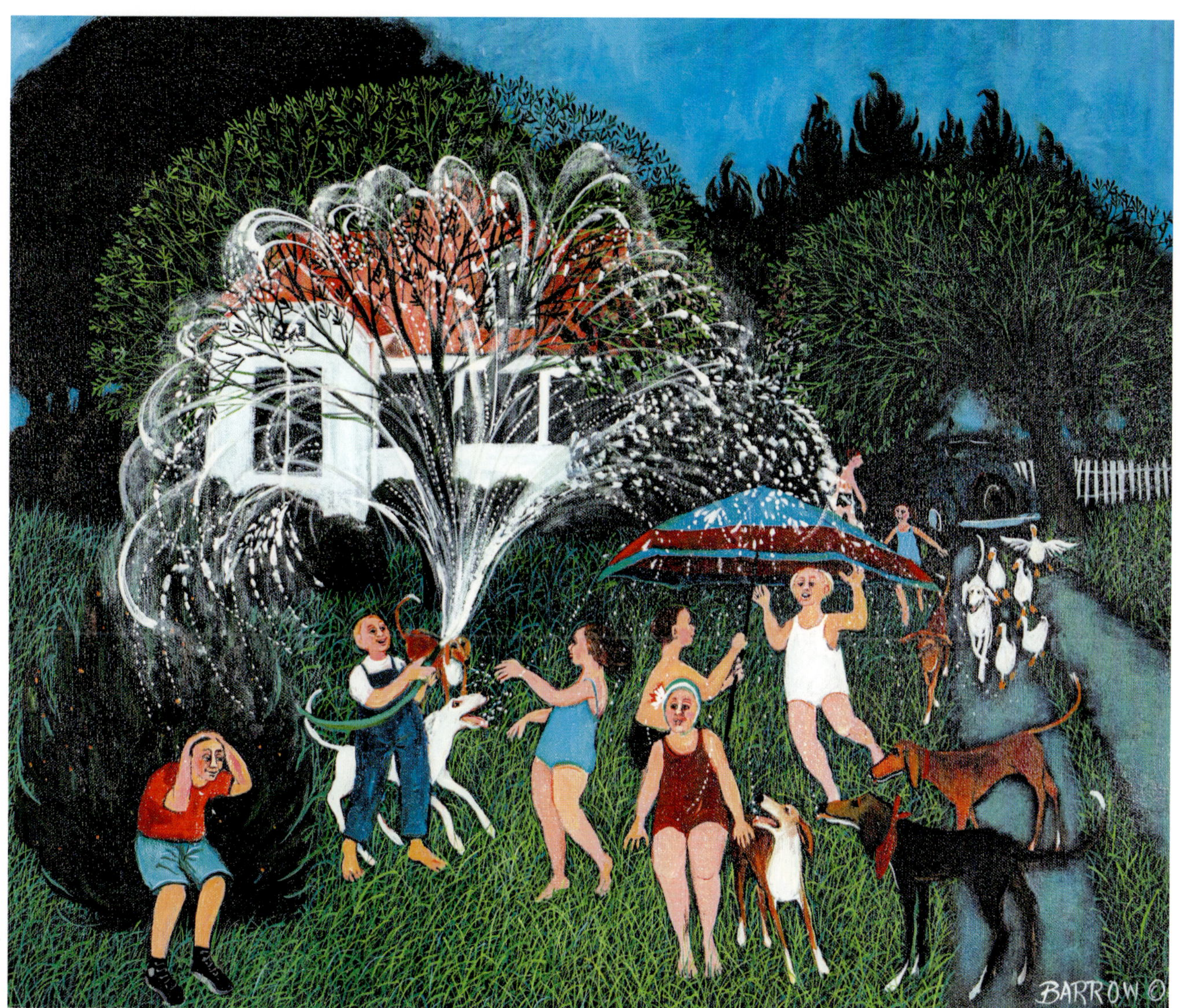

Summer Fun, n.d., oil on canvas, 20 × 24 inches. Private collection.

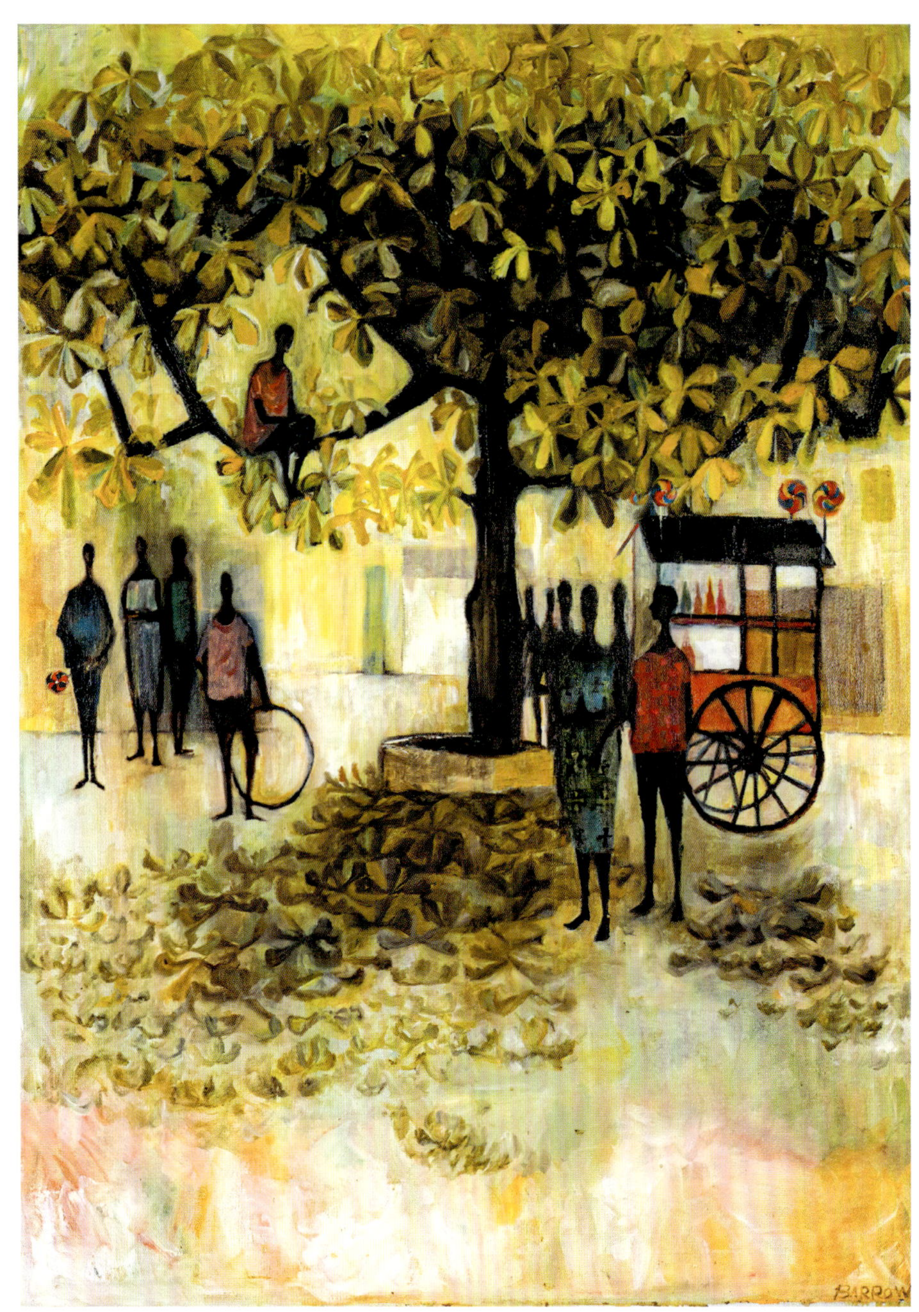

Zaccheus, n.d., oil on canvas, 36 × 26 inches.
Private collection.

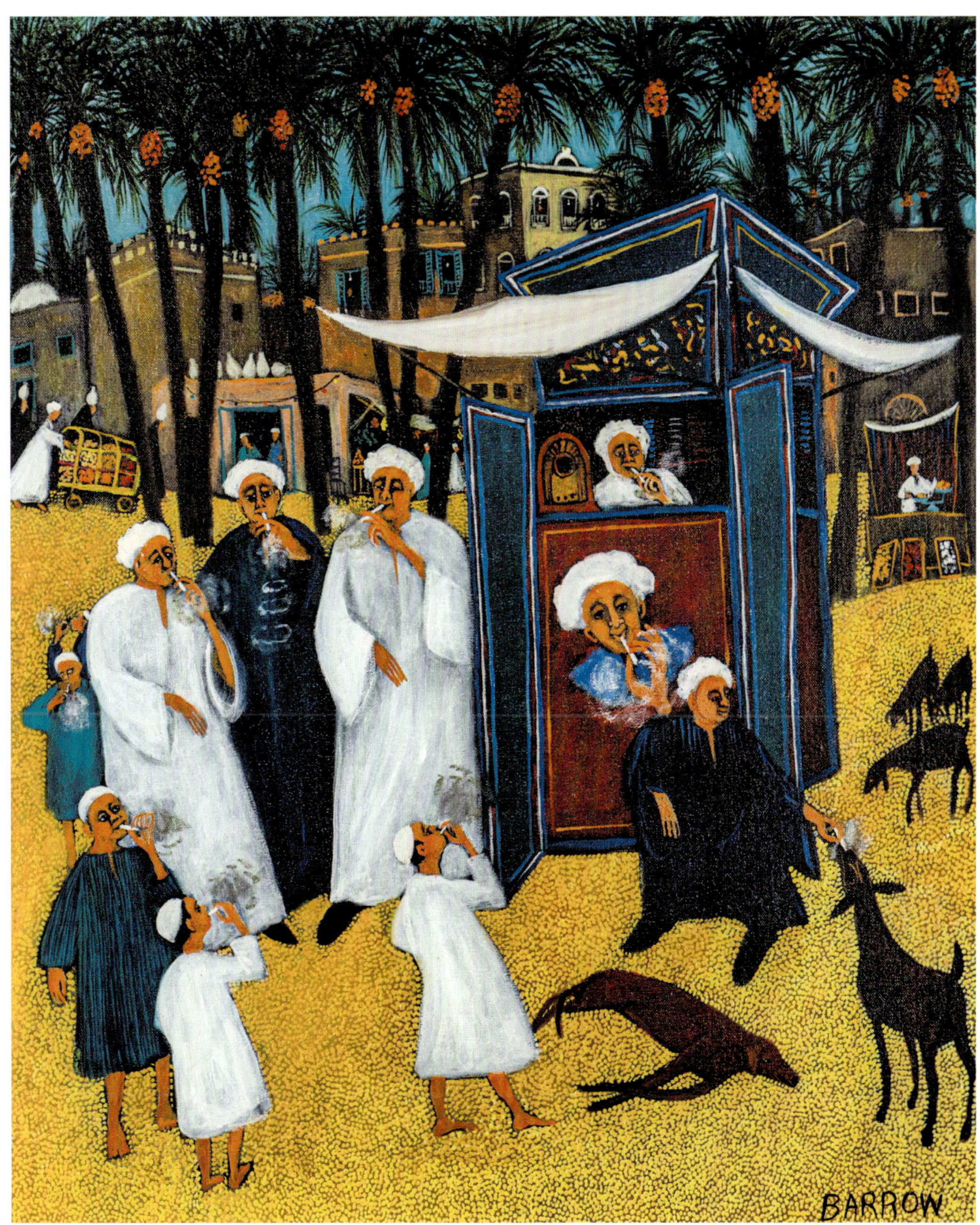

Smoking, n.d.,
oil on canvas, 21 × 25 inches.
Collection of David Barrow.

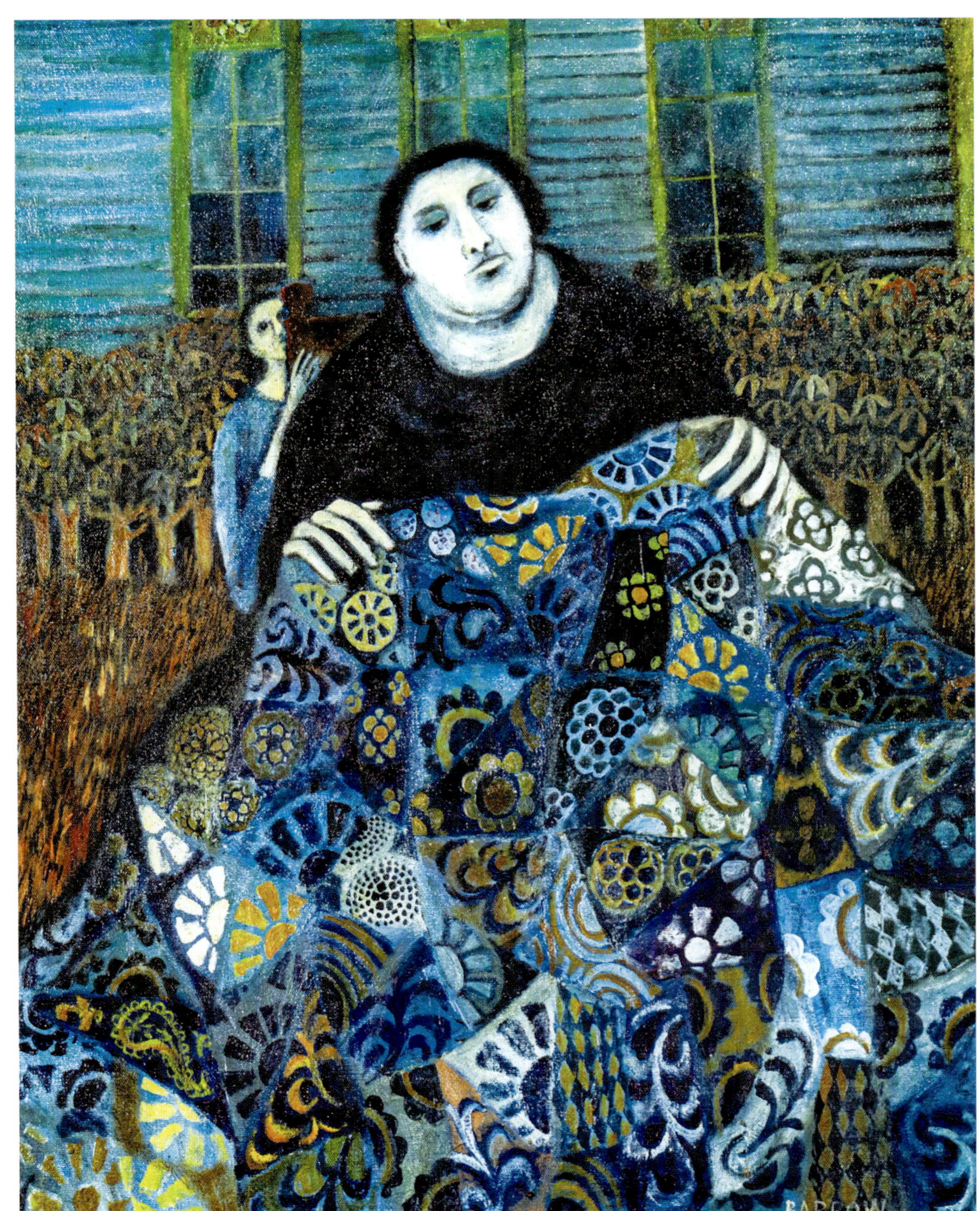

The Blue Quilt, n.d., oil on canvas, 21 × 25 inches. Collection of David Barrow.

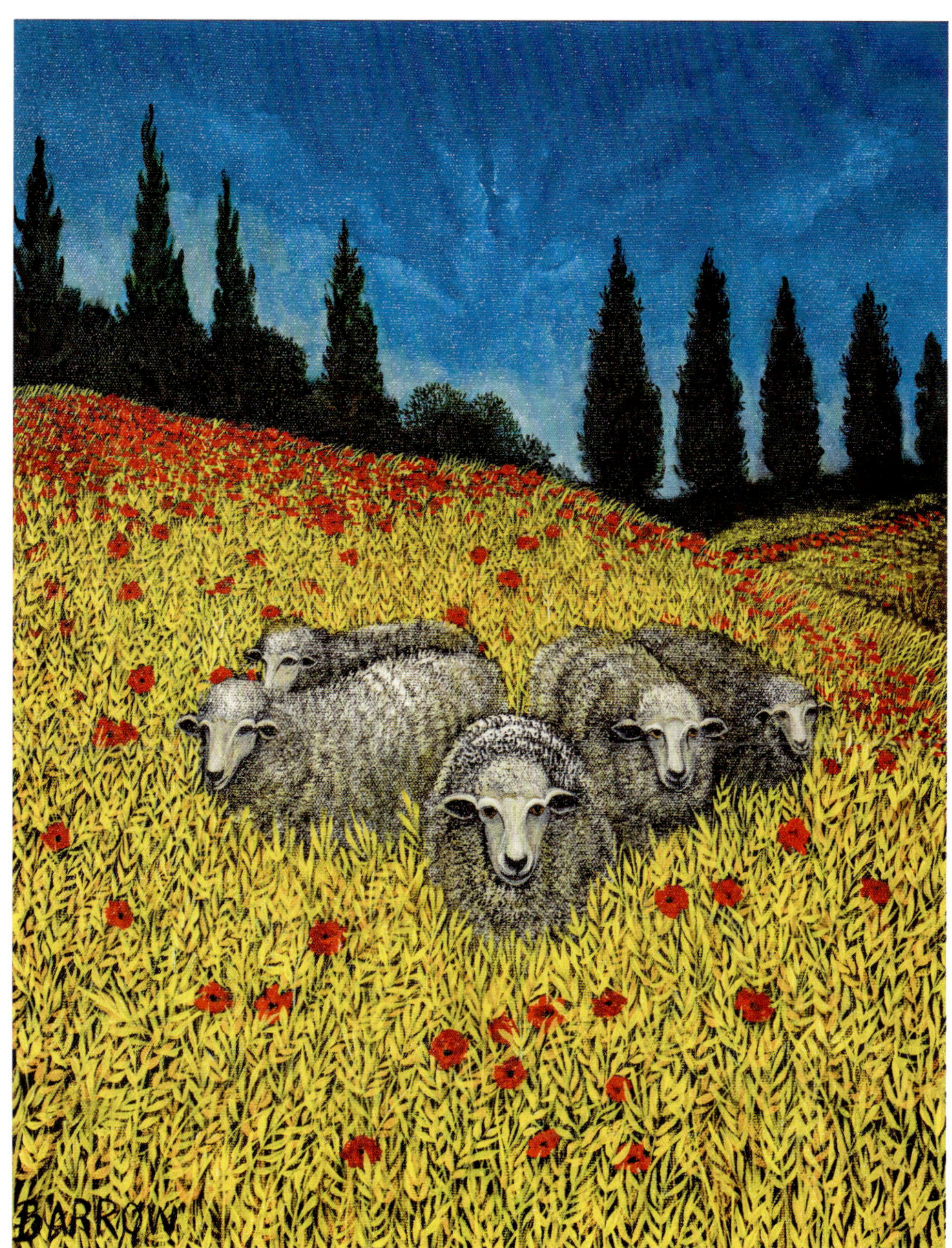

Sheep, n.d., oil on canvas, 21 × 17 inches.
Private collection.

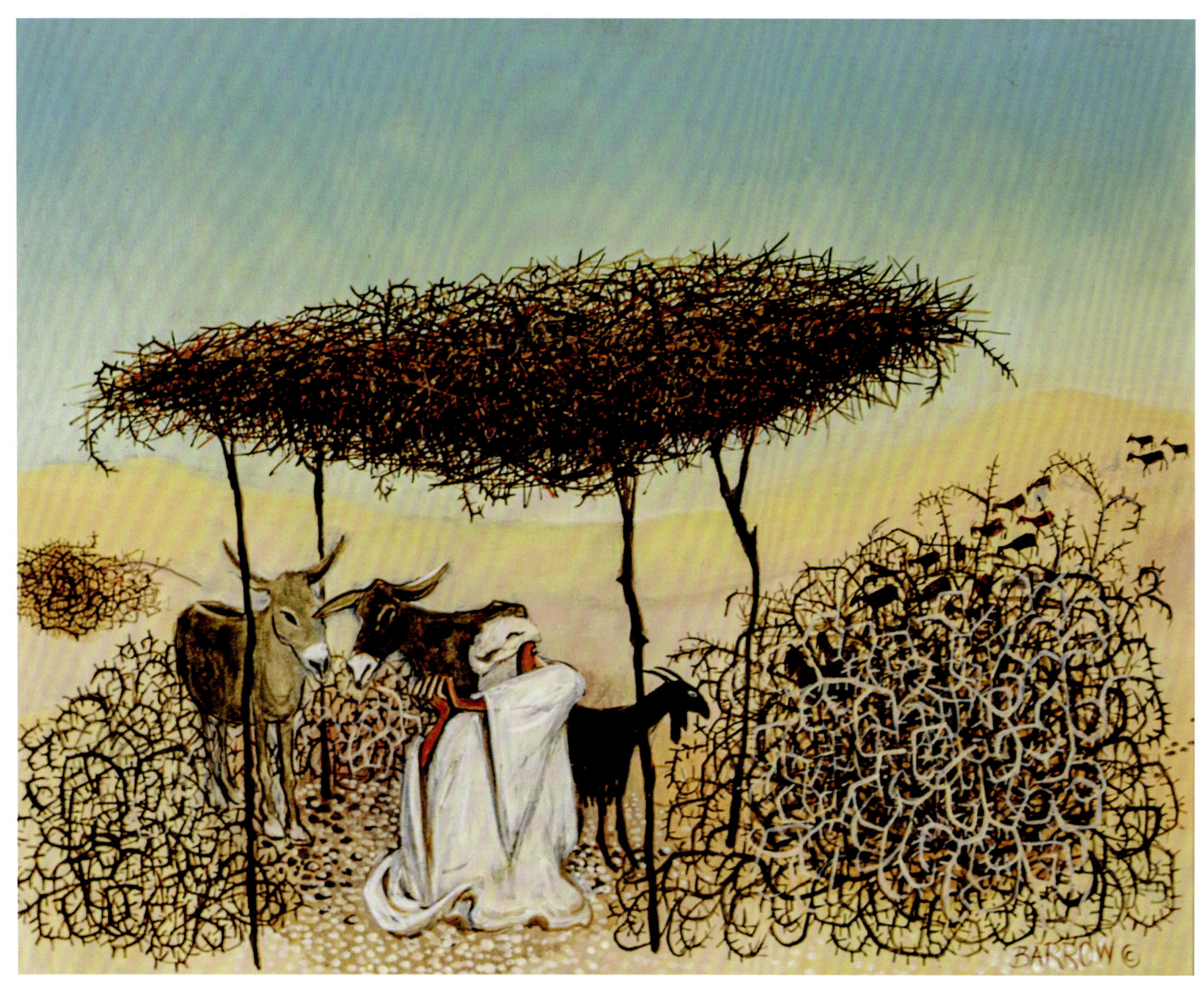

Jonah Beneath the Brush Arbor, n.d., oil on canvas, 18 × 22 inches. Private collection.

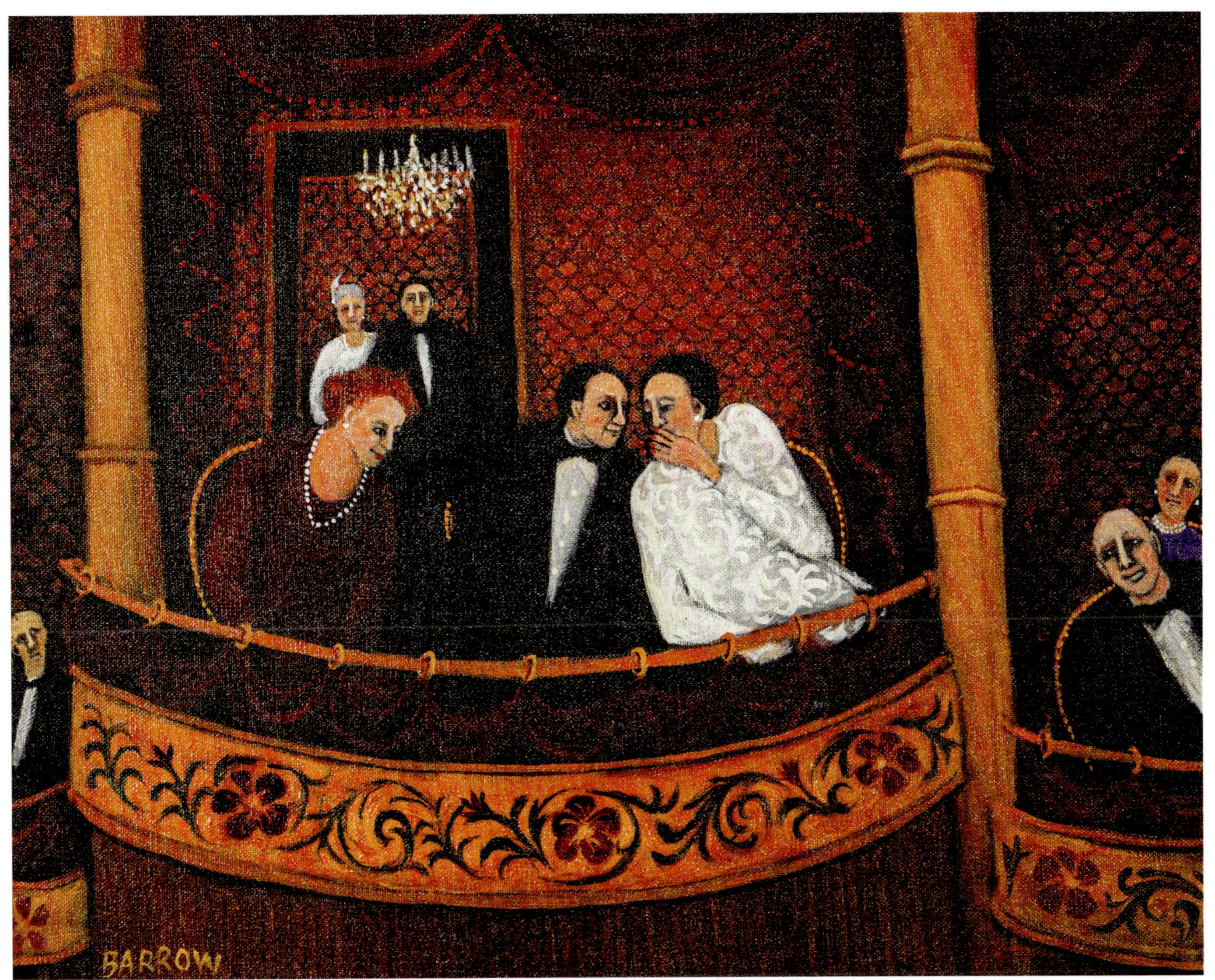

A Little Night Music, n.d., oil on canvas, 16 × 20 inches. Private collection.

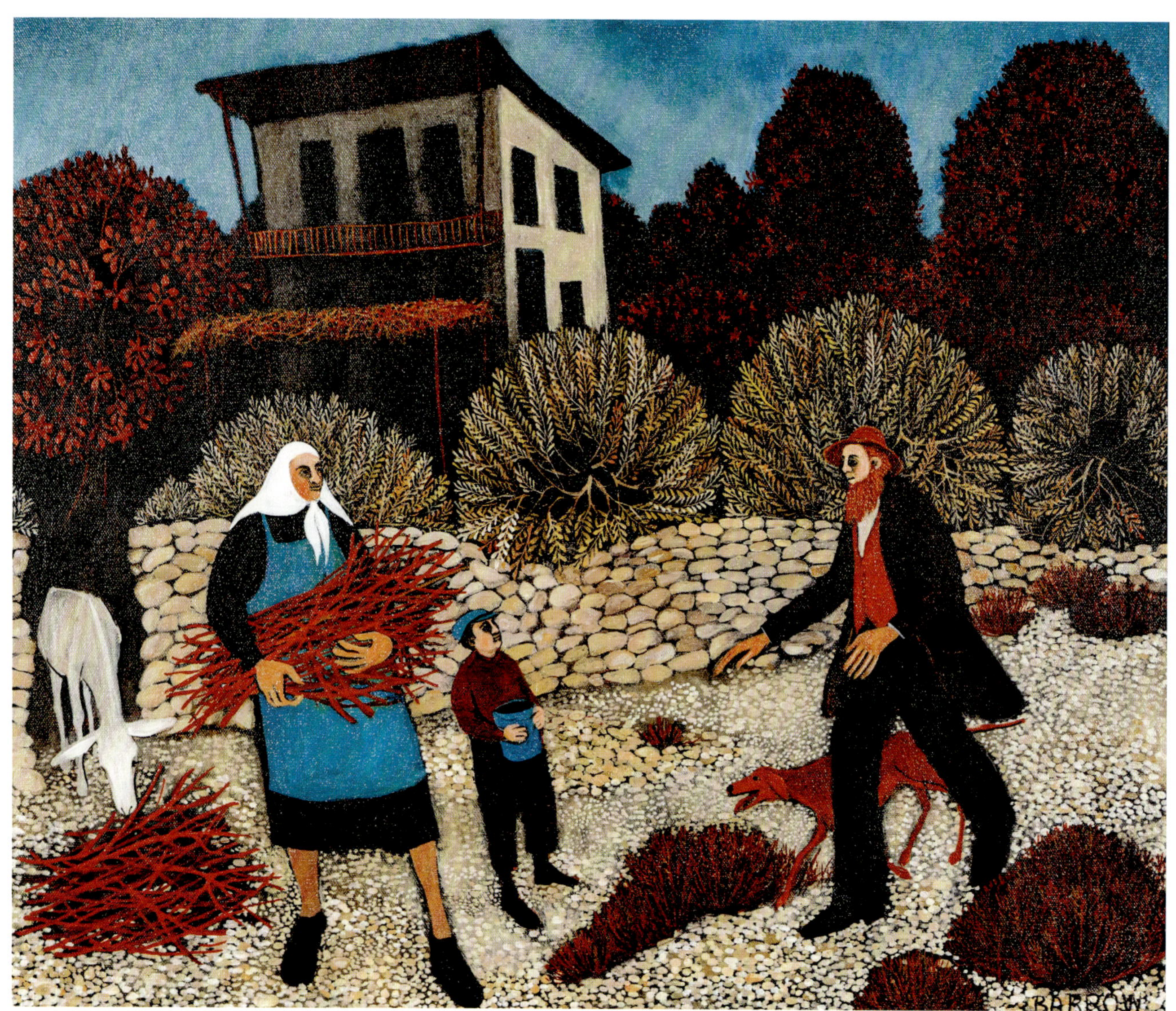

The Widow at Zarephath, Gathering Sticks, n.d., oil on canvas, 26 × 30 inches. Private collection.

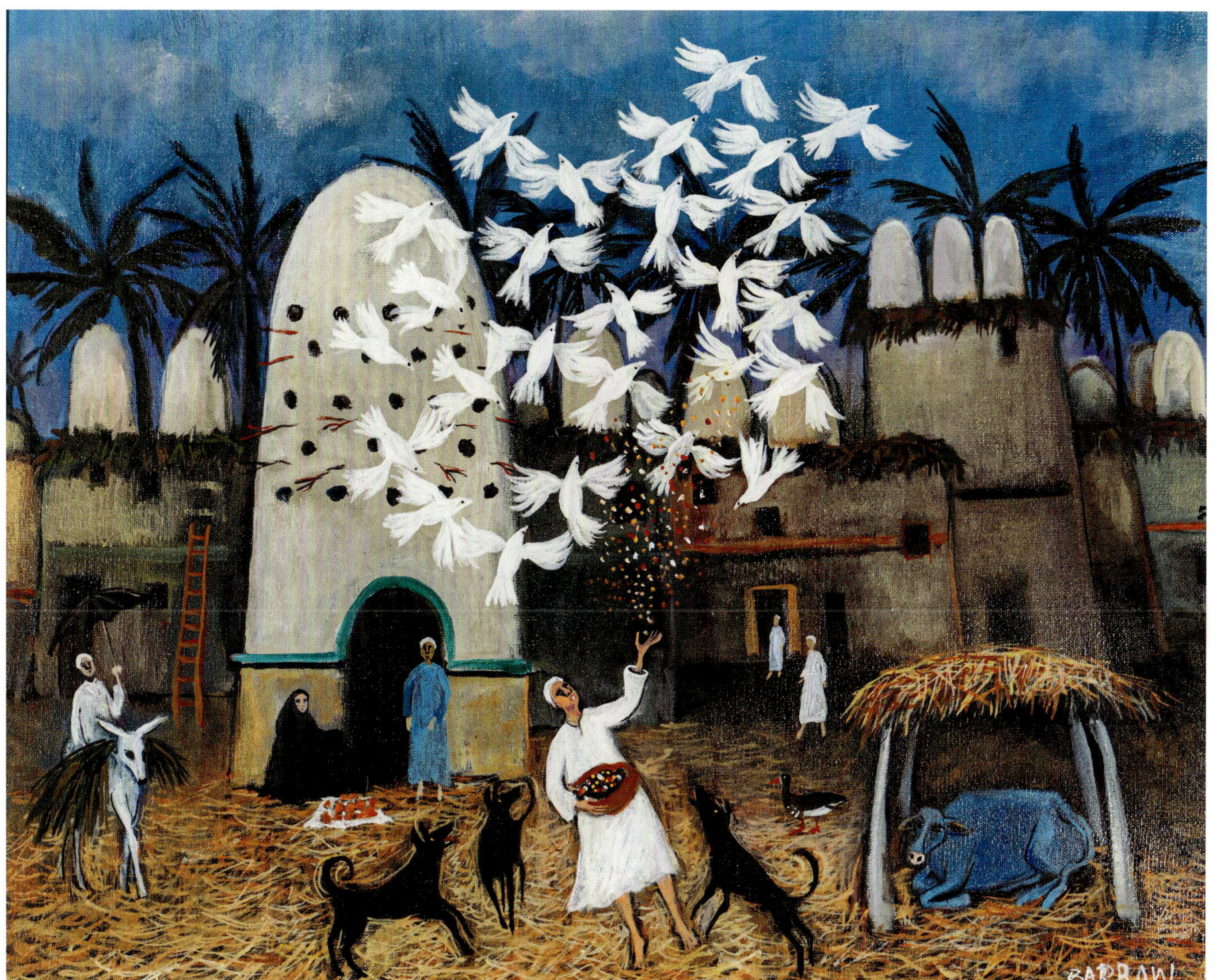

Feeding the Pigeons, n.d., oil on canvas, 20 × 24 inches. Private collection.

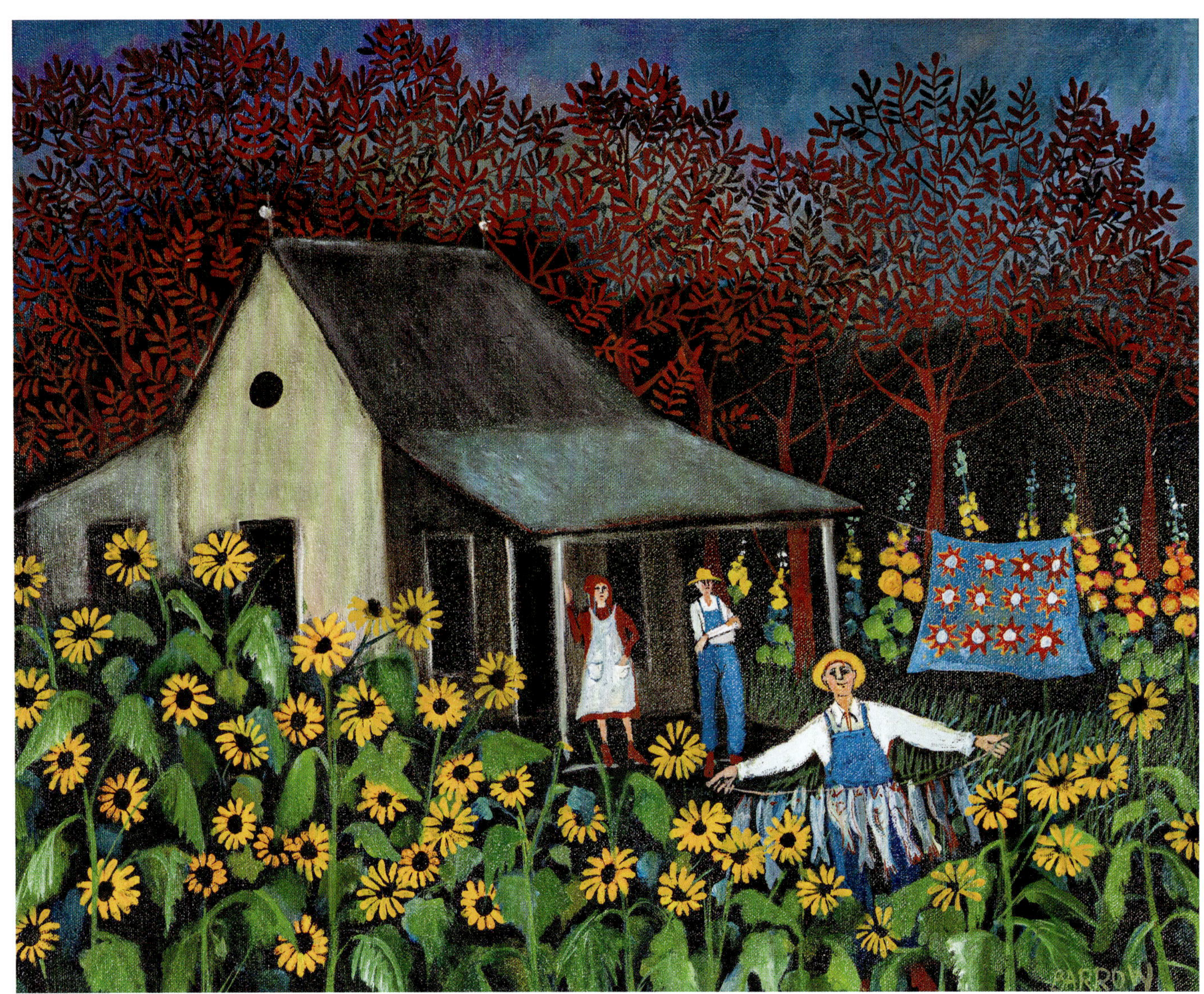

Jacob: The Calling, n.d., oil on canvas, 20 × 24 inches. Private collection.

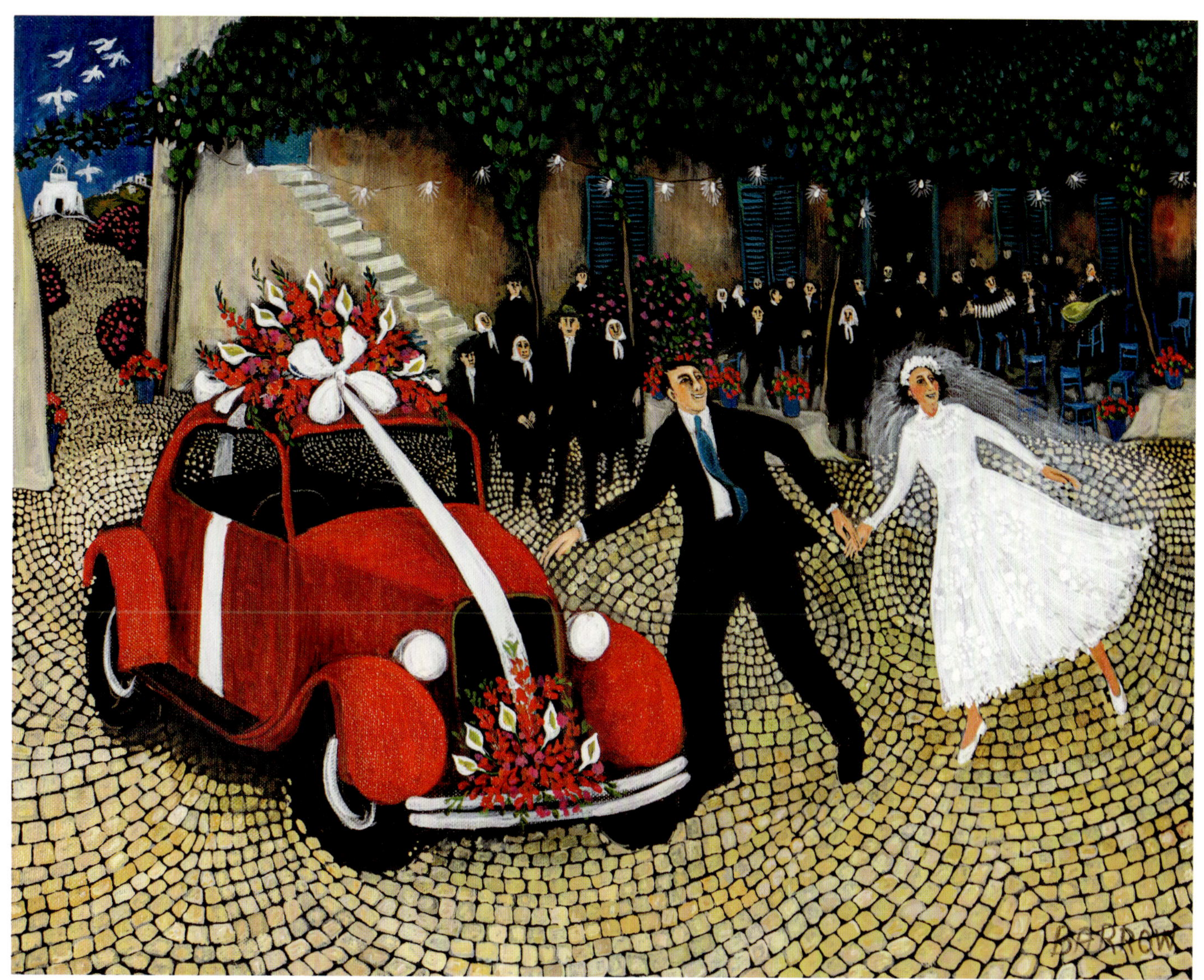

The Getaway, n.d., oil on canvas, 16 × 20 inches. Private collection.

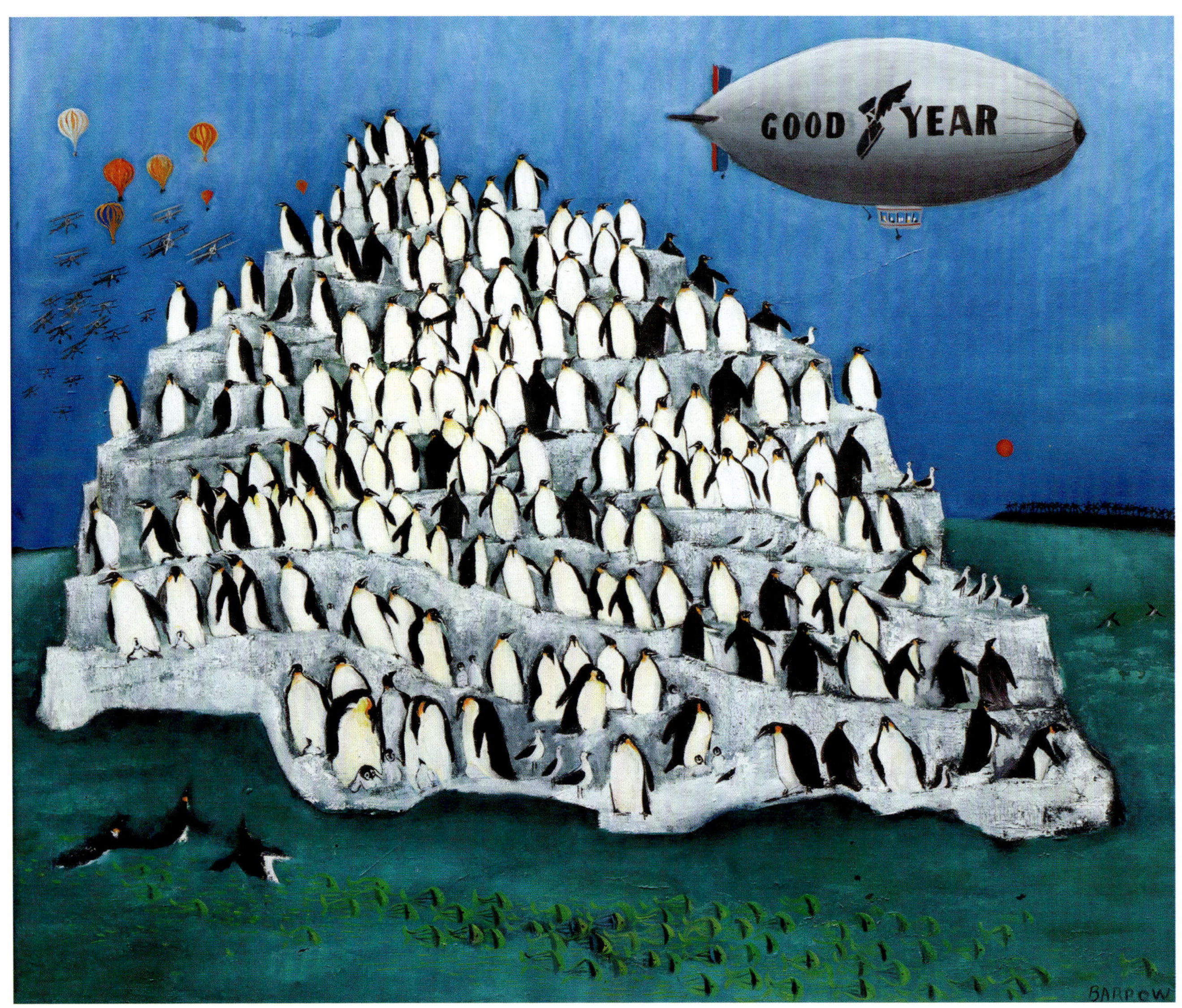

Penguins, n.d., oil on canvas, 30 × 36 inches. Private collection.

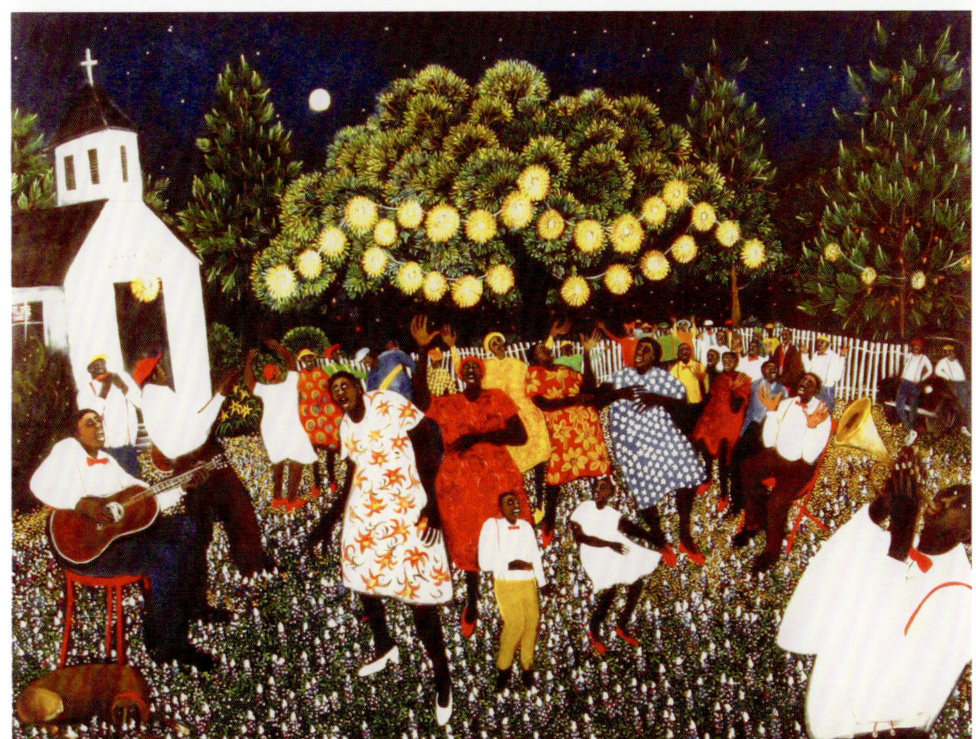

Hallelujah Time #2, ca. 1985, oil on canvas, 30 × 40 inches. Private collection.

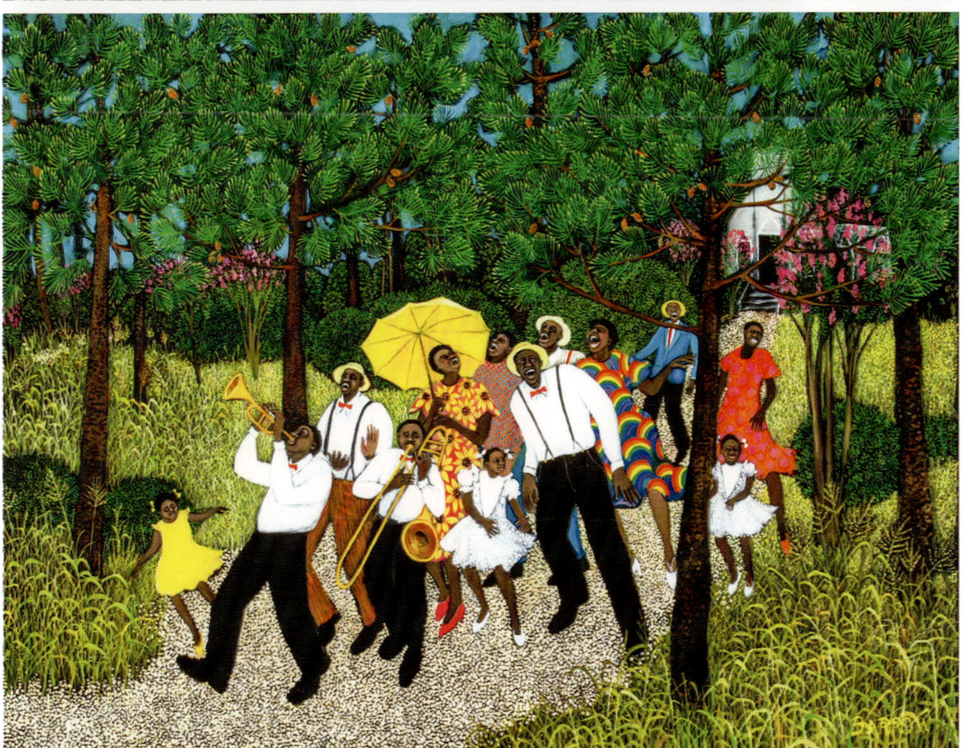

Oh Happy Day!, 1994, oil on canvas, 30 × 40 inches. Private collection.

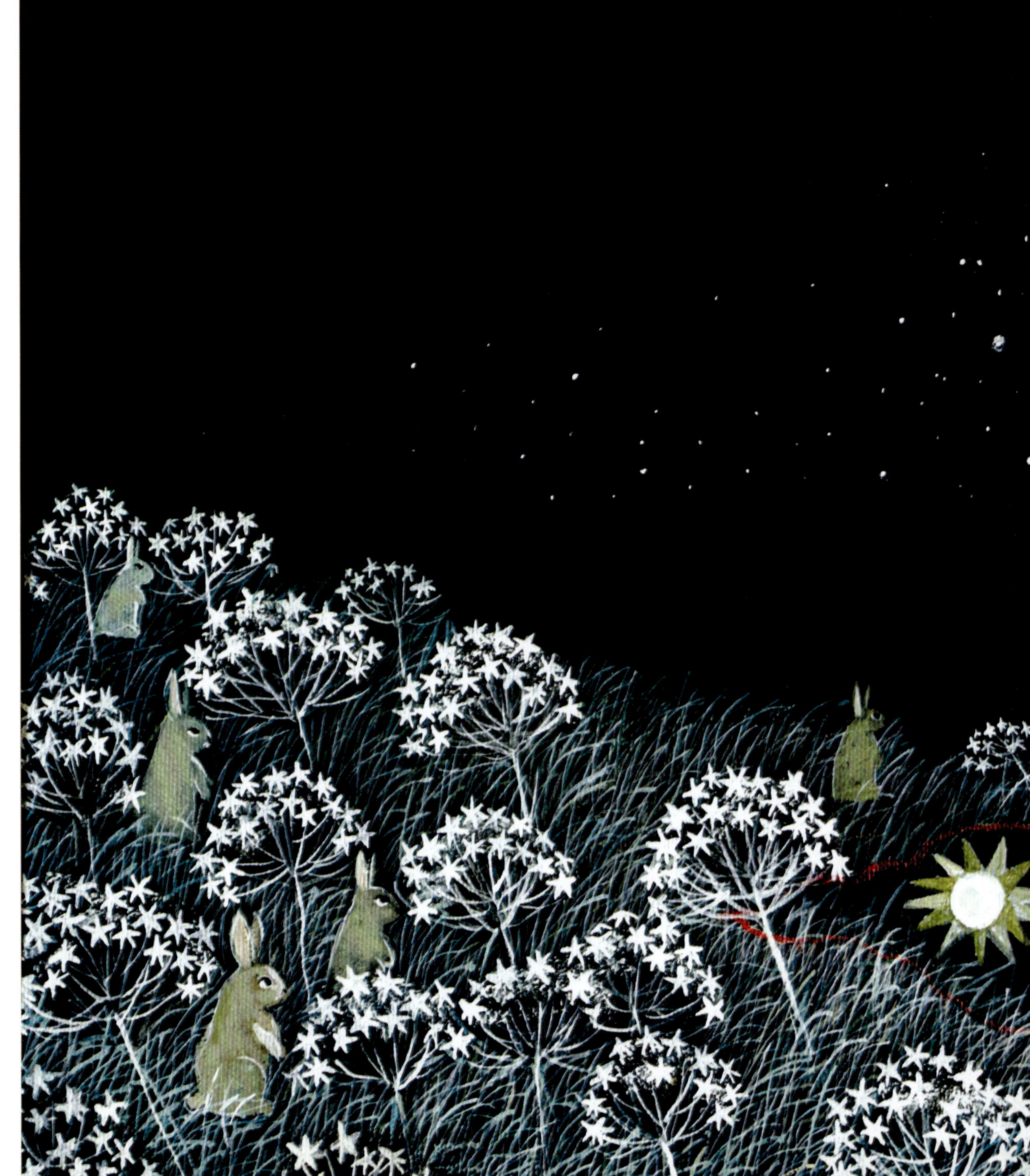

Life Between the Questions, n.d.,
oil on canvas, 13 × 25 inches.
Private collection.

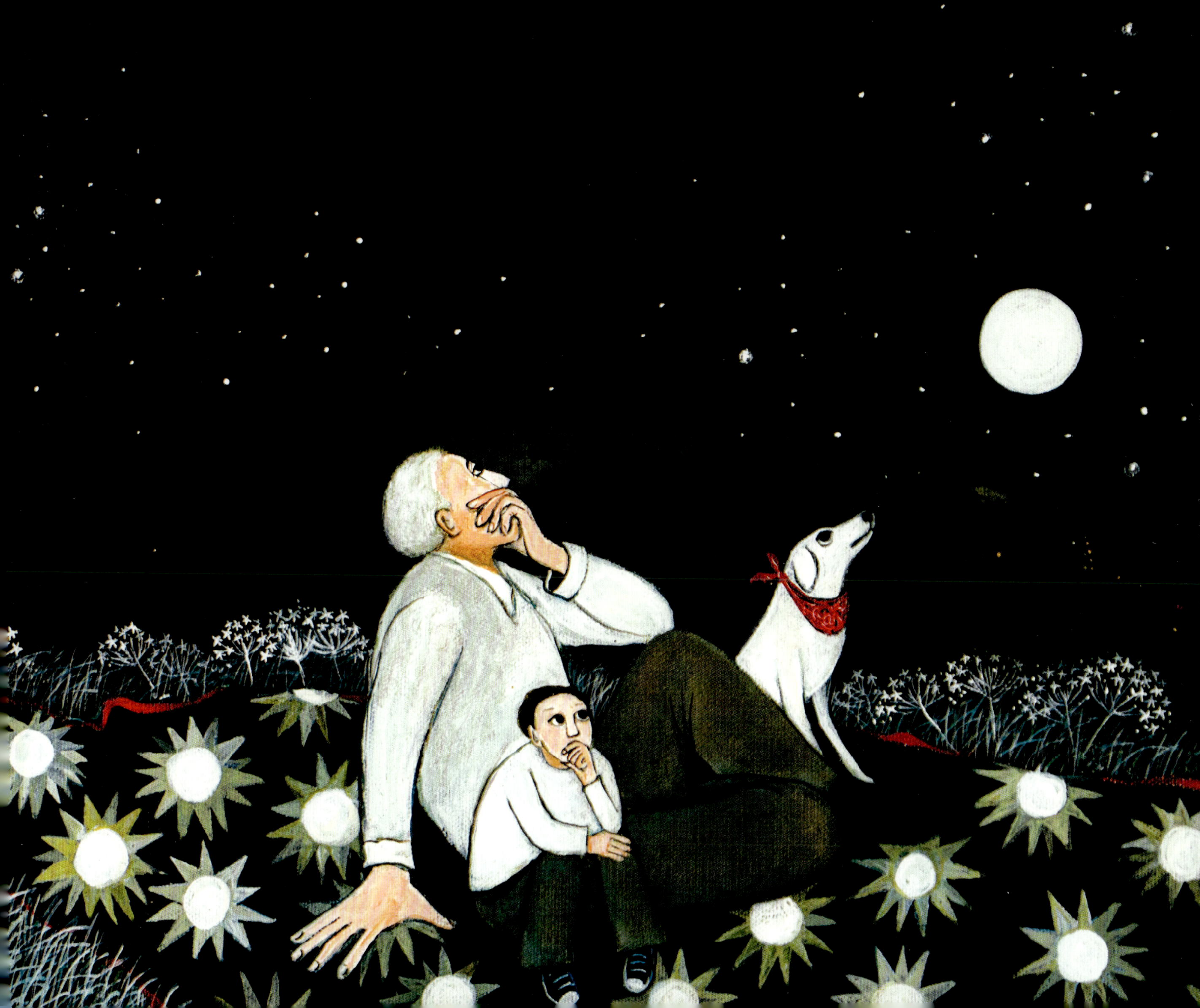

REMEMBRANCE

David Brown Barrow Jr.

In 1955 I received an architecture degree from the University of Texas and joined the United States Air Force to become a fighter pilot. In 1956 I was in the jet school at Laredo. I came home one weekend to see my parents, and one of my friends from architecture school called to invite me to a party that Saturday night at a house across Lake Austin.

I walked into a room with all the lights out, and the people were sitting around the walls in the dark. I looked across the room and saw a girl. The thought immediately popped into my mind: "That's the girl I'm going to marry!" I was introduced and it occurred to me that I should get to know this girl. The next several weeks I came to Austin again to get to know Lu Ann, who was about to get a degree in art from UT.

From Laredo, I went to fighter school in Glendale, Arizona, and now could talk to Lu Ann only by telephone or by letters. Before long, I asked her to marry me, and after I came in from flying one Friday, we were married in an Episcopal church in Glendale on December 7, 1956.

At the end of 1957 I accepted an offer to leave active duty for the reserves and we moved to Dallas, where I joined my mentor, Harwell Hamilton Harris, an internationally known California architect and former dean of the UT architecture school. Our son David III was born in Dallas in 1959. He lives in Austin with his wife, Laura Sikes Barrow, and our granddaughter and grandson, Angela Grace and Michael Thomas.

In 1961 we moved to Austin to start my architectural practice and participate with my father in designing and building Northwest Hills. Our son Thomas Edward was born in 1962. Thomas became a minimalist-style artist but unfortunately died in New York in 1995.

Moving around in the air force and then to Dallas and Austin, Lu Ann had never really had a place to settle down to pursue her art career. But now that we were settled in Austin, she did.

From 1965 to 1980 Lu Ann had a popular booth during the Fiesta at the Laguna Gloria Art Museum. She also had numerous solo exhibitions and participated in group shows. Later she showed at Wagner and Wunderlich Galleries. Since 1993 she has been represented by Valley House Gallery & Sculpture Garden in Dallas. In 2006 she had a solo retrospective show at the Austin Museum of Art. In 1999 Laura Bush asked her to do a poster for the Texas Book Festival and, in 2001, another one for the first National Book Festival. In 2019 she had a solo show at the Neill-Cochran House Museum in Austin.

The American architect Frank Lloyd Wright said that he didn't put pen to paper until he saw the proposed building in his head. Lu Ann didn't begin a painting until she saw it in her head.

In 2003 she wrote the following:

> From my university days to the present, my paintings have been narrative in a folkloric style using elements I've absorbed from childhood memories, from travels in Texas and the US, Europe, the Middle East and Mexico, from observing people and listening to their stories, and delighting in the presence of animals in our lives. . . .
>
> The tenor of my paintings is usually joyful and celebratory, with rare expressions of sorrow or even shadows. . . .
>
> In the 1970s I took an intensive two-year course of Bible study that opened an inexhaustible source of ideas and images in my mind. The paintings I've done from scripture do not look "biblical" or different from my secular subjects, because I dress the subjects in clothes that are closer to our time in settings that are familiar to the viewer today. I think that secular and sacred are often seamless and that my biblical paintings are visual parables which must still work in regard to color and composition. . . .
>
> For me, painting is a language I've been blessed with and can use to gather what I've seen, read, heard, or experienced and share it with the viewer, a way to say visually, "Let me tell you . . ."

Lu Ann and I had a long and happy life together. Over the years many people have told her how much happiness she had brought into their lives in person or through her paintings. If you would like to see some of Lu Ann's paintings, you can look on the website of Valley House Gallery & Sculpture Garden or you can go downstairs at St. Matthew's Episcopal Church in Austin, Texas, to see sixty-two feet of them (on mattress cardboard!) that she did for fun for an event there. Now, of course, you can also leaf through the pages of this book.

When we first met the Vogel family at Valley House, they spent some time looking at her paintings. Then Donald Vogel, the founder, who I had heard was very selective about whom he represented, said, "David, come into the next room and sit down with me." I did, and he said, "We've got someone special here."

We really did.

ACKNOWLEDGMENTS

The genesis of this book was an art festival at St. Matthew's Episcopal Church in Austin, Texas, in September 2022 to exhibit the work and honor the life of gifted parishioner Lu Ann Barrow.

A committee of dedicated church members and others made the event and all the goodness possible: Alina Ramos-Wasmuth, Allen Keith, Anne Webster, Babs Clendenin, Betsy McCraine, Cathey Roberts, David Barrow, Emily Hansen, Hink Johnson, Isabel Bursk, Joyce Statz, Kimberly Upchurch, Leslie Kjellstrand, Linda Fryer, Lisa Richardson, Mary Nell Frucella, Sharon Roberts, Valorie Bray, Sharon Lowe, Kelly Sonnen, Kevin McGillicuddy, Carlana Stone, David Kupfer, Sandra Bravo, Jenny Bailey Watson, Kate Canby, Avery Goodgame, Diane Sparks, Norma Lambert, Pat Naeve, Janet Fulk, David Kennedy, and Jill Miller.

Cathey Roberts expertly headed up the photographing of all the paintings. Allen Keith was there to take pictures of people and activities and generally do whatever, whenever.

The following trusting souls loaned paintings to the show: David Barrow, Gidget Fisher, Mary Nell Frucella, Elaine Goessling, Chuck Huffman, Meta Butler Hunt, Hink Johnson, Pat and Chuck Naeve, Kathleen and Frank Niendorff, Dedee and Steve Norman, Susan and Jack Robertson, Archie Robinson, Joyce Statz, Dot and Sherm Strance, Donna Thomas, Kay White, Kay and Leon Whitney, and Blythe and Chris Wilson. On learning about this book, others wished to have the paintings they owned included as well: Mary Jo Culver, Charles M. Peveto, and Susan and Bryan Roberts.

The festival culminated in a musical and literary performance featuring Jane Michael reading her poem "Joy to the World"; the Reverend Chuck Huffman joined by daughters Heather and Laura singing "Taste and See"; Leah Knight-Schumacher singing "His Eye Is on the Sparrow"; Debra and Marc Eyck making their musical magic; the Reverend Chanta Bhan reading an essay; and the St. James Missionary Baptist Church choir and accompanists performing several selections, including "Oh Happy Day!" when they invited audience participation—and got it!

This volume also includes thoughtful essays by the Reverend Dr. Susan Barnes, priest and art historian; David Barrow, husband of the artist; Ginger Henry Geyer, visual artist; Karen Pope, PhD, art history professor; and Cheryl Vogel, owner of the gallery representing Lu Ann's work for three decades. The essays are engaging and enlightening and all have different perspectives.

From the moment the idea for a festival was put forth, David Barrow enthusiastically gave his support in every way.

All of the above folks have our profound thanks for the roles they played in bringing this project to fulfillment. In the truest sense, this was a labor of love for and delight in the woman who shared our lives for a while and enriched them forever.

What cannot fail to be mentioned is the central and very supportive role taken on by Texas A&M University Press, particularly that of Thom Lemmons, editor in chief (truly an editor's editor).

My gratitude is almost overwhelming.

INDEX